Data Patterns

patterns & practices

Philip Teale, Microsoft Prescriptive Architecture Guidance

Christopher Etz, Simple Fact

Michael Kiel, Simple Fact

Carsten Zeitz, Simple Fact

ISBN 0-7356-2200-0

Contents

Chapter 3

Data Movement Patterns   23

Preface

Welcome to *Data Patterns*. This guide briefly introduces patterns and describes a new organizational approach that categorizes them according to various viewpoints and relationships. The guide then presents 12 patterns that span several of these viewpoints, and explains how they can be integrated into an enterprise data solution.

Increasingly, software design professionals are using patterns to efficiently share the important architectural tradeoffs and design decisions they make while architecting and building enterprise solutions. Christopher Alexander first used patterns to describe architecture and design in his book, *The Timeless Way of Building*; however, his patterns were for towns, buildings, and rooms. Software design professionals soon recognized the value of patterns as a language for sharing design experiences.

Over the past decade, the burgeoning patterns community has discovered patterns in many areas of system architecture and software development. This book embraces the continuing work of the patterns community and extends it by showing how to apply patterns using Microsoft® SQL Server™.

Early feedback from database professionals has confirmed that patterns are invaluable tools for sharing expertise. Patterns give developers and architects a common language to help bridge the gap between their two disciplines. The authors hope these patterns prove useful to you and that you will contribute to the growing patterns community. There is much more work to be done.

Who Should Read This Book

Most readers of this book should fall into one of the following categories:

- Database designers, database administrators, data administrators, architects, designers, and developers who are new to patterns
- Database designers, database administrators, data administrators, architects and designers who are already experienced in using patterns to build data solutions

For those in the first group, the first two chapters are very important in helping you understand why and how you should use patterns. These chapters are essential in understanding these data patterns. You are likely to discover that you have implemented some of these patterns before without knowing that they were patterns.

Readers in the second group are familiar with most of the content in Chapter 1, "Data Patterns." Chapter 2, "Organizing Patterns," introduces new material on how Microsoft is organizing its pattern repository. Most of the patterns in Chapters 3 will be familiar to you; however, the implementation examples provided should help you apply them to SQL Server.

How This Book Is Organized

Chapter 1, "Data Patterns," introduces the notion of a pattern, explains how a pattern documents simple, proven mechanisms, and shows how collections of patterns provide a common language for developers and architects. To illustrate these concepts, this chapter applies abbreviated versions of actual patterns to real-life development situations.

Chapter 2, "Organizing Patterns," explains how patterns emerge at different levels of abstraction and across a variety of domains. This chapter explores pattern levels in detail and outlines an organizing frame that helps you find relevant patterns quickly. The chapter then demonstrates how patterns provide a vocabulary to efficiently describe complex solutions without sacrificing detail.

Chapter 3, "Data Movement Patterns," describes architecture, design, and implementation patterns related to how to create and manage copies of data to efficiently to fulfill your solution requirements. The current set of patterns discusses the topic of data replication as a means of meeting data needs, such as providing local copies of data to distributed or intermittently-connected applications, or for other purposes such as disaster recovery.

Appendix A, "Patterns and Pattlets," lists all of the patterns and pattlets defined in this pattern catalog. *Pattlets* are actual patterns to which this guide refers, but which it does not discuss in detail. The concept of pattlets is discussed in Chapter 2, "Organizing Patterns."

These data patterns use many data terms the meaning of which may vary from case to case. The Glossary is designed as a convenient reference to these terms.

Documentation Conventions

This guide uses the following style conventions and terminology.

Table 1: Style Conventions Table

Element	Meaning
Bold font	Objects, classes, methods, predefined functions, and events.
Italic font	Names of patterns and pattlets referenced in this guide. New terminology also appears in italics on first use.
`Monospace font`	Code examples.
Note	Alerts you to supplementary information.
Hint	Alerts you to supplementary information that is helpful, but not essential to the task at hand.

Community

The patterns in this guide are part of a new Patterns community on GotDotNet. GotDotNet is a Microsoft .NET Framework Community Web site that uses workspaces in an online collaborative development environment where .NET developers can create, host, and manage projects throughout the project life cycle. You can also use this Patterns community to post questions, provide feedback, or connect with other users for sharing ideas.

Access to the Patterns community is available at *http://gotdotnet.com/team/architecture /patterns.*

Feedback and Support

The authors would appreciate your feedback on this material. In particular, they would be grateful for any guidance on the following topics:

- Is the information that is presented in this guide useful to you?
- Is this information presented in the correct sequence and with the appropriate level of detail?
- Are the chapters readable and interesting?
- Overall, how do you rate the material?

Send your feedback to the following e-mail address: pnppatfb@microsoft.com. Please be aware that this is not a technical support alias; to obtain technical support for Microsoft products and technologies, visit *http://support.microsoft.com.*

The patterns documented here are designed to jump-start the architecture and design of enterprise applications. Patterns are simple mechanisms that are meant to be applied to the problem at hand and are usually combined with other patterns. They are not meant to be plugged into an application. Example code is provided "as is" and is not intended for production use. It is only intended to illustrate the pattern, and therefore does not include extra code, such as exception handling, logging, security, and validation. Although this deliverable has undergone testing and review by industry luminaries, it is not supported like a traditional Microsoft product.

Acknowledgments

Many thanks to the following advisors who provided invaluable assistance:

- Ward Cunningham, Cunningham & Cunningham, Inc.
- Martin Fowler, ThoughtWorks, Inc.
- David C. Hay, Essential Strategies, Inc.
- Ralph Johnson, University of Illinois at Urbana-Champaign

Thanks also to the many contributors who assisted us in the production of this book, in particular:

- Mohammad Al-Sabt, Microsoft Prescriptive Architecture Guidance
- Michael Blythe, SQL Server User Experience
- Matthew Evans, Microsoft Prescriptive Architecture Guidance
- Mike Ferguson and Colin White, Intelligent Business Strategies, Inc.
- Sanjeev Garg, Satyam Computer Services
- Steve Kirk, MSDN
- Susan Filkins, Entirenet
- Prem Mehra; Customer Advisory Team, SQL Server Development
- Oliver Sims, Sims Associates

Finally, thanks to the companies that agreed to participate in our user experience test:

- Subrata Biswas
- Mark Carpenter and Vic Martindale
- Brian Monahan and Tony Williamson, Standard Life Assurance Company
- Helen Townsend, Reuters
- Dave West, Barclays Bank

1

Data Patterns

"…since my intention is to write something useful for anyone who understands it, it seemed more suitable to me to search after the effectual truth of the matter, rather than its imagined one." — Niccolo Machiavelli in *The Prince*, 1532

Although managing data gets less fanfare than other IT disciplines, it is crucial to the well-being of enterprise systems. The architecture, design, and implementation of data management systems are also very complex. The goal of data patterns is to directly address this complexity, and provide solutions to common problems, often using relatively simple mechanisms. These patterns are based on "the effectual truth," as Machiavelli called it, which means that they are based on approaches to solving the problems that have proven successful.

Data professionals have been working with data patterns for many years, but they have probably not explicitly recognized this. Until now, very few data patterns have been formally captured and shared with a wider community. Instead, they continue to be held within organizations as tacit knowledge, or expressed in the form of internal standards or guidelines.

These patterns are about the problems faced by those who build the data services in an enterprise class business solution. They address the need to create the database designs and the data services that exist invisibly to the applications that use the data; in other words, the data and services that exist within the data ecosystem.

Patterns are useful to data professionals because they:

- Document simple mechanisms that work.
- Provide a common vocabulary and taxonomy for developers and architects.
- Enable solutions to be described concisely as combinations of patterns.
- Enable reuse of architecture, design, and implementation decisions.

The rest of this chapter introduces the notion of data patterns, explains how a pattern documents simple, proven mechanisms, and shows how collections of patterns provide a common language for developers and architects. To illustrate these concepts, this chapter applies abbreviated versions of actual patterns to real-life data situations.

Patterns Document Simple Mechanisms

A pattern describes a recurring problem that occurs in a given context and, based on a set of guiding forces, recommends a solution. The solution is usually a simple mechanism, a collaboration between two or more data objects, services, processes, threads, components, or nodes that work together to resolve the problem identified in the pattern.

Note: Although the underlying mechanisms described in these patterns are conceptually simple, in practice their implementation can become quite complex. The implementation requires skill and judgment to tailor general patterns to fit specific circumstances. In addition, the pattern examples in this chapter are highly abbreviated for the purpose of introduction; the actual patterns in subsequent chapters are much more detailed.

Consider the following example:

You are building a laptop solution which contains an application that salespeople use to give customers quotations for orders (OrderQuote). It is important that the applications can work in a disconnected environment. The salespeople, therefore, require local data services on their laptops (for example, CustomerDetails, Orders, Price, Products, and BusinessRules tables). It is important that the quotations are as accurate as possible. It is also important that a quote given by any particular laptop application is consistent with one that another laptop would produce within a defined period of time. How do you structure your design so that your local data is sufficiently current and any work done is consistent within a defined time period no matter which laptop it is performed on?

A simple solution to the OrderQuote problem is to create a parameterized data replication service that copies only the required data to a particular laptop on a periodic basis. The parameters identify the data requirements of a particular salesperson. The data is copied from a shared database on a server. In cases where the same data is required on more than one laptop, a master copy of that data is taken at a point in time and then it is copied to all laptops to ensure consistency of application results.

It is likely that you have solved problems like this in a similar manner, as many other designers have. If you have, you were providing data copies in a manner that this guide identifies as the *Master-Slave Snapshot Replication* design pattern.

Patterns as Problem-Solution Pairs

The *Master-Slave Snapshot Replication* pattern does not mention an OrderQuote process, or CustomerDetails tables. Instead, the pattern looks something like the following abbreviated example.

Comparing the abbreviated pattern example in Figure 1.1 (on the next page) with the solution outlined above illustrates the difference between the pattern, which is a generalized problem-solution pair, and the application of the pattern, which is a very specific solution to a very specific problem. The solution, at a pattern level, is a simple, yet elegant, collaboration between data stores. The general collaboration in the pattern applies specifically to a data replication service, which provides the mechanism that controls the copying of the data. Clearly, you can apply the same pattern to countless situations by modifying the pattern slightly to suit specific local requirements.

Written patterns provide an effective way to document such simple and proven mechanisms. Patterns are written in a specific format, which is useful as a container for complex ideas. As Figure 1.1 shows, a pattern is defined as a three-part relationship between a general problem, its context, and its solution, which is based on real-world experience, and is documented in a consistent, formal structure.

Although pattern writers usually provide implementation examples within these generalized patterns, it is important to understand that there are many other correct ways to implement these patterns. The key here is to understand the guidance within the pattern and then customize it to your particular situation. For example, the implementation examples provided in this guide are based on Microsoft® SQL Server™. If you need to implement the pattern using a different product, you can do so. However, an implementation that is optimized for another database management system might look quite different, and while these two implementations could differ significantly, both would be correct.

Master-Slave Snapshot Replication

Context

You are designing a replication solution for the following requirements:

 • An entire replication set is to be replicated from a single source to one or several targets.

 • Changes to the target data which may have occurred since the last transmission will be overwritten by a new transmission.

Problem

How do you move an entire replication set from source to target so that is consistent at a given point in time?

Solution

Make a copy of the source replication set at a specific time (this is known as a *snapshot*), replicate it to the target and overwrite the target data. Thereby all changes on the target replication set are dropped and replaced by the new source replication set.

A *Snapshot Replication* uses a single replication building block, consisting of the source, the replication link with Acquire, Manipulate and Write, and the target as shown.

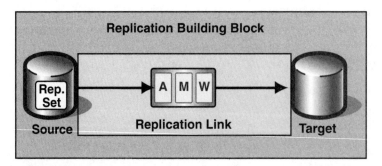

Figure 1.1
Master-Slave Snapshot Replication pattern, abbreviated

Patterns at Different Levels

Patterns exist at many different levels of abstraction. Consider another example, this time at a higher level of abstraction than design:

> You are architecting a common approach to be the basis for how you move copies of data around in your organization. You have to deal with data that is held on many different platforms, is structured in different schemas, has policies and constraints on its relationships, has differing security requirements, has different application uses, and has different operational characteristics. How do you organize your data copying at a high level to be flexible, loosely coupled, and yet sufficiently cohesive?

The *Move Copy of Data* architecture pattern describes a solution to this problem, which involves using one fundamental architectural building block to solve the problem. The block reflects that fundamentally, the solution always consists of a source data store that contains the data to be copied and moved; a link across which it moves and which contains the same three basic services; and a target data store where the copy is to be held. The block is expressed as a pair-wise solution, but it can be applied, fractal-like or in a network-structure, to solve data copy problems of varying complexity. When you do this, you need to maintain discipline about the knowledge of the resulting copy infrastructure so you can understand the provenance of copied data and the impact of changing parts of it. Again the common approach helps you to solve this problem, but it does not do it for you.

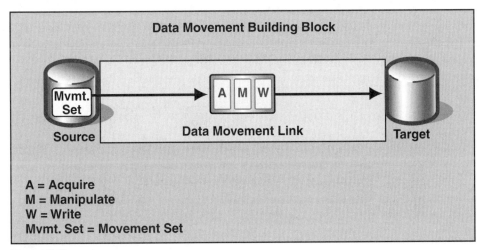

Figure 1.2
Data Movement Building Block

If you always architect data movement systems this way, then you employ this pattern already. Even so, there are many reasons why you might want to understand the patterns that underpin this architectural approach. You may be curious about why systems frequently are built this way, or you may be looking for more optimal approaches to problems that this pattern does not quite resolve. In either case, it is worth examining the patterns and mechanisms at work here.

The reason that this approach is so commonly used is that it deals with complexity well by using a layered approach to dividing up the problem. In this case, the layers are instances of the source-target pairings (where the pairings are not constrained to 1:1 relationships). This simple strategy of organizing to manage complexity helps to solve two challenges: the management of dependencies and the need for exchangeable parts. Building environments without a well-considered strategy for dependency management leads to brittle and fragile solutions, which are difficult and expensive to maintain, extend, and substitute. *Enterprise Solution Patterns Using Microsoft .NET* contains an architectural pattern called *Layered Application*, which contains a more detailed explanation of the benefits of a layered approach.

Simple Refinement

As you will see in later chapters, *Master-Slave Snapshot Replication* is a refinement of *Master-Slave Replication,* which is in turn a refinement of *Move Copy of Data.* This means that the context, forces, and solution identified in *Master-Slave Replication* still apply to *Master-Slave Snapshot Replication*, but not the other way around. That is, the *Master-Slave Replication* pattern constrains *Master-Slave Snapshot Replication*, and the *Master-Slave Snapshot Replication* pattern refines the *Master-Slave Replication* pattern. This pattern relationship is useful to manage complexity. After you understand one pattern, you must only understand the incremental differences between the initial pattern and patterns that refine it. Another example should help to illustrate the concept of refinement:

> The laptop application that you built has been very successful and its use is expanding. Also, the company is extending it products and services. Now you want to copy data to more laptops and the amount of data required is larger. Currently, you deliver all the data that the laptop application needs every time you replicate. Continuing with your present strategy would put an unacceptable load on the infrastructure. How do you provide the data copies to the expanded customer base within the constraints if your infrastructure?

One solution to this problem is to extend *Master-Slave Replication* by adding an additional capability: the ability to deliver only the changes that have occurred at the server to the copied data since the last replication to the target. Any unchanged data is not copied again. If the percentage of data that is changed between replications is relatively low, this solution works well. One solution for this is captured in *Master-Slave Transactional Incremental Replication.*

Notice the relationships between these patterns (see Figure 1.3). *Move Copy of Data* introduces a fundamental strategy for moving copies of data. *Data Replication* and *Master-Slave Snapshot Replication* progressively refine this idea and constrain it to a certain type of one-way replication that replaces all of the data at the target. *Master-Slave Transactional Incremental Replication* refines *Master-Slave Replication* to different type where only data changes are copied.

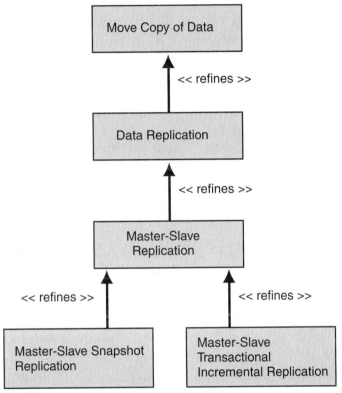

Figure 1.3
Refinement of related patterns

Adding functions to specific layers is not the only way to manage this growing complexity. As complexity warrants, designers often create additional layers to handle this responsibility. For example, some designers would instead choose to adopt a layered approach to the infrastructure problem by adding intermediary copy stores into the infrastructure. This allows the data to be copied out in waves first to the intermediary stores and then to the set of laptops serviced by each intermediary. This solution is described in the *Master-Slave Cascading Replication* pattern.

When grouped together, these variations form part of a cluster of patterns (see Figure 1.4) that visually represents common approaches to copying data. Clustering, used in this context, simply means a logical grouping of some set of similar patterns and their relationships. Usually the relationship is one of refinement, as shown above. Other relationships can be added, however. This guide adds a relaxed relationship, which means "can use." So *Master-Master Replication* can use *Master-Slave Snapshot Replication*, but there is no refinement between the patterns. This notion of a cluster is quite useful for expanding the view of patterns to encompass an entire solution, and for identifying clusters of patterns that address similar concerns in the solution space. Chapter 2, "Organizing Patterns," discusses clusters in more detail.

Common Vocabulary

While considering the *Move Copy of Data*, *Data Replication*, *Master-Slave Replication*, *Master-Slave Snapshot Replication*, *Master-Slave Transactional Incremental Replication*, and *Master-Slave Cascading Replication* patterns, you probably noticed that patterns also provide a powerful vocabulary for communicating software architecture and design ideas. Understanding a pattern not only communicates the knowledge and experience embedded within the pattern, but also provides a unique, and hopefully evocative, name that serves as shorthand for evaluating and describing software design choices.

For example, when designing a data copy environment, a developer might say, "I think the pricing information should be copied using *Master-Slave Snapshot Replication* and deployed using *Master-Slave Cascading Replication*." If another developer understands these patterns, he or she would have a very detailed idea of the design implications under discussion. If the developer did not understand the patterns, he or she could look them up in a catalog and learn the mechanisms, and perhaps even learn some additional patterns along the way.

Patterns have a natural taxonomy. If you look at enough patterns and their relationships, you begin to see sets of ordered groups and categories at different levels of abstraction. Chapter 2 further expands and refines this taxonomy.

Over time, developers discover and describe new patterns, thus extending the community body of knowledge in this area. In addition, as you start to understand patterns and the relationships between patterns, you can describe entire solutions in terms of patterns.

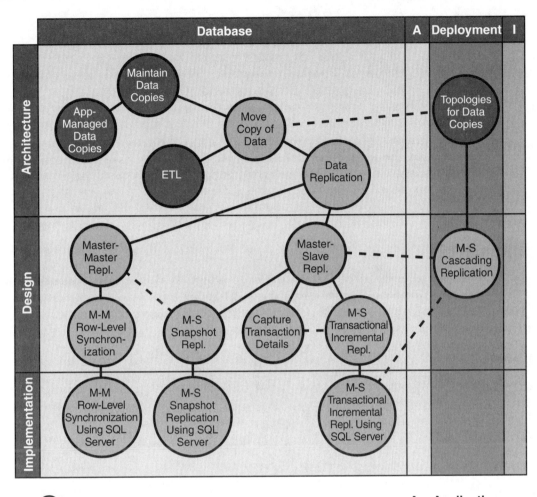

Figure 1.4

A cluster of data patterns

Concise Solution Description

In this guide, the term solution has two very distinct meanings: first, to indicate part of a pattern itself, as in a problem-solution pair contained within a context; second, to indicate a business solution. When the term business solution is used, it refers to a software-intensive data processing system that is designed to meet a specific set of functional and operational business requirements. A software-intensive data processing system implies that you are not just concerned with software and data; you must deploy this software and data onto hardware processing nodes to provide a holistic technology solution. Further, the software under consideration includes both custom-developed software and purchased software infrastructure and platform components, both of which have data needs and all of which you integrate together.

Summary

This chapter introduced the concept of a pattern, explained how patterns document simple, proven mechanisms, and showed how patterns provide a common language for designers and architects. Chapter 2 explains how to organize your thinking about patterns, and how to use patterns to describe entire solutions concisely.

2

Organizing Patterns

"Each pattern then depends both on the smaller patterns it contains, and on the larger patterns within which it is contained." — Christopher Alexander in *The Timeless Way of Building*

An innovation in one area of technology often fuels a breakthrough in another area. Radar technology turned into a cooking device: the microwave oven. The Internet itself was originally designed as a military communications network with resilience against single points of attack and has since turned into the world's largest repository of knowledge. Similarly, patterns, originally applied to building and town architecture, were quickly embraced by the software development community as a means to describe complex software systems.

Today there are dozens of patterns related to software with more emerging daily. This abundance of patterns creates a new set of challenges. How can a developer identify those patterns that are most relevant to the task at hand? Is the collection of patterns sufficient to describe complete solutions?

This chapter answers some of these questions by demonstrating how to:

- Identify relationships between patterns.
- Group patterns into clusters.
- Identify patterns at various levels of abstraction.
- Apply patterns to multiple aspects of a solution.
- Organize patterns into a frame.
- Use patterns to describe solutions concisely.

Pattern of Patterns

One reason the object-oriented programming community embraced patterns so emphatically is because patterns describe relationships. The base element of object-oriented programming is a class. However, a single class is not very meaningful apart from its relationship to other classes that make up the solution. In the same way, the data world is full of elementary items and their relationships. These could be entities and attributes, database tables related by foreign keys, original data and copies of it, and so on.

A pattern about an elementary item is valuable in its own right. But patterns that pull other patterns together are even more powerful. These pattern clusters turn the sea of individual patterns into a much more manageable collection of patterns by highlighting the relationships between the clustered patterns. For example, to implement *Master-Master Replication,* you first need to build an exact copy of one of the masters, and you could use *Master-Slave Snapshot Replication* to do that. Then you would have to manage the integrity of the two masters, and you could use *Master-Master Row-Level Synchronization* for this purpose. So these three patterns form at least part of a useful cluster.

Patterns participate in other relationships, too. For example, some patterns are refinements of others. *Master-Master Row-Level Synchronization* is a specific application of the concept of *Master-Master Replication.*

To begin organizing patterns according to relationship, visualize a set of patterns as small circles (see Figure 2.1):

If you draw a line between each pair of patterns that share some relationship, you get a picture like the one in Figure 2.2.

The somewhat random collection of circles in Figure 2.2 becomes a connected web of patterns. When you look at a pattern, you can now identify closely related patterns and review those as well. You can also identify "neighborhoods" of closely related patterns and see how they are related to other, more remote patterns.

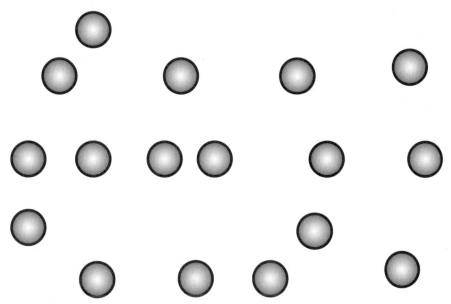

Figure 2.1
A set of patterns

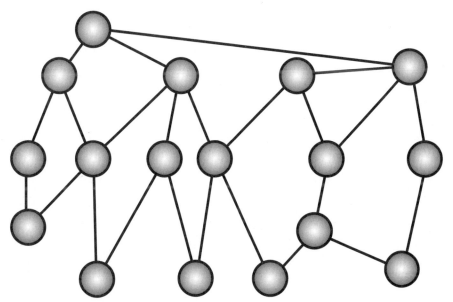

Figure 2.2
Pattern relationships represented as lines

Pattern Clusters

Charting the relationships between patterns helps you navigate from one pattern to a set of related patterns. However, it does not yet tell you where to start. If you are building a data replication solution, should you look at *Master-Slave Snapshot Replication* first or *Master-Slave Transactional Incremental Replication*? A cluster gives you hints on what to read first by clearly identifying a root for the set. Pattern clusters are groupings of patterns that relate to a specific subject area. So in this example, you might need to read either *Master-Slave Replication* or *Data Replication* or *Moving Copy of Data* depending on how much you've already thought through the issues at the architecture or design levels.

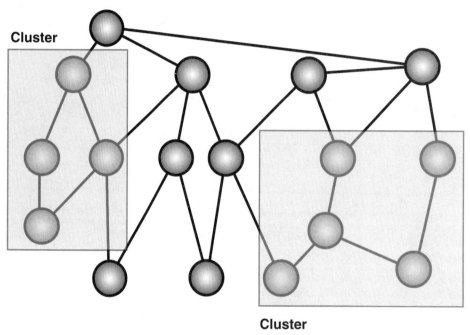

Figure 2.3
Pattern clusters

This first release of Microsoft® Data Patterns identifies a Data Movement patterns cluster, with the *Move Copy of Data* pattern at its root. Industry luminaries and customers identified these patterns as having critical importance right now.

Different Levels of Abstraction

Dividing patterns into clusters makes them more manageable. However, recognizing levels of abstraction by dividing the patterns in a hierarchy from general to more specific detail is also very useful. It not only categorizes patterns so that people with different roles can find the patterns that correspond most closely to their area of interest, but also helps you decide which patterns to consider first. A cluster is then a hierarchy of patterns with the root pattern at the top.

A good way to categorize the patterns is to divide the pattern graph into the three levels shown in Figure 2.4.

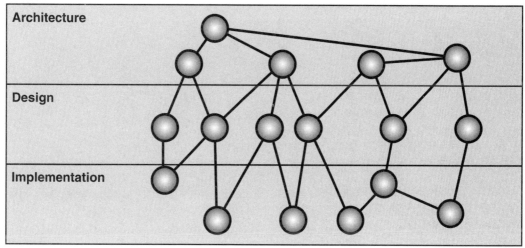

Figure 2.4
Levels of abstraction

Architecture Patterns

The data architecture patterns express the highest-level design patterns for data topics. They are completely product-independent and are not meant to be directly implemented.

Design Patterns

The data design patterns provide a greater level of design detail, while still remaining product-independent. However, they are usually detailed enough to serve as the basis for a product-specific implementation pattern.

Implementation Patterns

The patterns community refers to more detailed, programming-language-specific patterns as idioms. This definition works well for software patterns. However, the scope of this guide is not just software, but software-intensive systems, including the deployment of the software onto hardware processing nodes to provide a holistic business solution. Therefore, Microsoft modifies the definition of an idiom given in Pattern-Oriented Software Architecture (POSA) [Buschmann96] to reflect the broader scope and relabels these patterns as implementation patterns:

> An implementation pattern is a low-level pattern specific to a particular platform. In the case of the data patterns, we describe how to implement data design patterns with SQL Server.

Viewpoints

Although the levels of abstractions help to address different user groups, they do not reflect the fact that a software solution encompasses other viewpoints and special-izations. Each viewpoint itself can also focus on different levels of abstraction. Therefore, Microsoft patterns depict the following viewpoints as vertical slices across the pattern graph: database, application, and infrastructure. There is often a significant gap between the application and infrastructure viewpoints. Concepts, abstractions, and skill sets are sufficiently different to warrant the insertion of a buffer between the two that helps to bridge the divide. This viewpoint is called the deployment viewpoint.

This line of reasoning results in the four viewpoints shown in Table 2.1.

Table 2.1: Patterns Viewpoints

Viewpoint	Description
Database	The database view describes the persistent layer of the application. This view looks at such things as logical and physical schemas, database tables, relation-ships, and transactions.
Application	The application view focuses on the executable aspect of the solution. It includes such things as domain models, class diagrams, assemblies, and processes.
Deployment	The deployment view explicitly maps application concerns to infrastructure concerns (for example, processes to processors).
Infrastructure	The infrastructure view incorporates all of the hardware and networking equip-ment that is required to run the solution.

Figure 2.5 overlays these viewpoints as vertical lines over the pattern graph and the levels of abstraction.

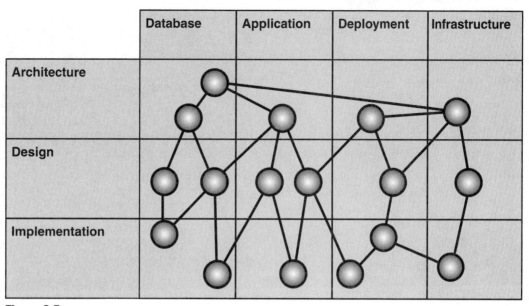

Figure 2.5
Adding viewpoints

Keep in mind that these four areas describe different viewpoints of the overall solution. Therefore, unlike the levels of refinement, these viewpoints do not describe a hierarchy, but provide four different ways of looking at the solution. You can compare these viewpoints to different types of maps. One map of a region may depict traffic networks such as roads and freeways, while another map of the same area shows the topography. Still another map may show state and county borders. Each map has its own vocabulary. For example, lines in the topographical map represent elevations, while lines in the traffic map represent streets. Nevertheless, all maps describe the same subject: a specific geographic region.

For the sake of simplicity, Figure 2.5 does not show the cluster boundaries. However, the clusters, the layers of abstraction, and the viewpoints exist in parallel. They represent different ways to access the same set of patterns.

The Pattern Frame

The combination of three levels of refinement on the vertical axis and the four viewpoints on the horizontal axis results in a grid-like organization of the pattern graph. Figure 2.6 on the next page shows this arrangement, which is called the *Pattern Frame*.

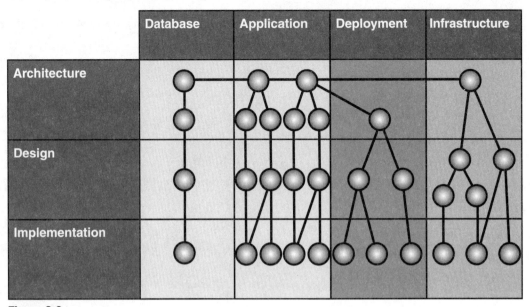

Figure 2.6
The Pattern Frame

The Pattern Frame is included with each individual pattern description as a point of reference and as a navigational aid.

Constraints

Because there are so many potential patterns in the data realm, it is necessary introduce a means to constrain the set that is being developed at any point in time. Figure 2.7 shows a simple view of electronically held data in an Enterprise context.

Terminology may vary, but generally within an Enterprise there are four main types of data stores:

- Operational data, which supports the daily customer-facing business processes.
- Informational data, which supports business reporting, analysis, and planning.
- Knowledge, which is the explicit storing of best practices and other forms of intellectual capital.
- Metadata, which is data about data, or the knowledge of what data is stored in the other three stores, how it is structured, and how it is used.

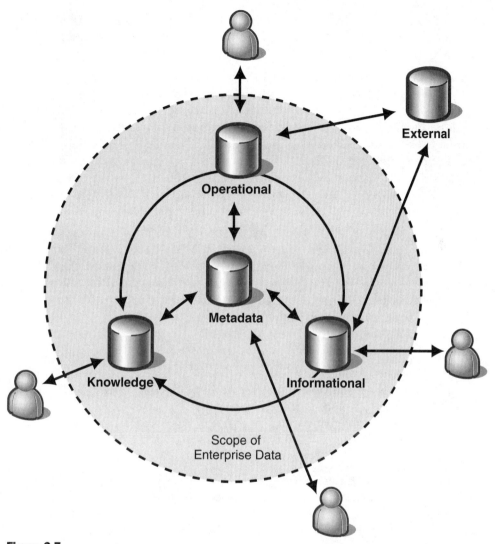

Figure 2.7
Principle enterprise data types

Different types of users interact with all these types of data stores, either to use them for business purposes or to administer and maintain them. They do this with tools, application packages, or customer applications.

These stores also interact as indicated by the arrows in Figure 2.7. Typically, operational data is copied to other operational stores, to informational stores, or to knowledge stores. Informational data is also copied to other informational stores and to knowledge stores.

In the context of this overall data ecosystem, this initial data patterns release focuses on how to move copies of data within the operational stores in Figure 2.7, and in certain contexts, also between the operational and informational stores.

The topic of moving copies was chosen because of the complexity of the problem today. This complexity has compounded as enterprise data processing has evolved from a single copy of data in a centralized database with offline nighttime batch work to distributed systems requiring constantly available data copies, and to data warehouses, Extract, Transform, and Load (ETL) services, and Relational Database Management Systems (RDBMS). The first set of patterns presented in Chapter 3, "Data Movement Patterns," is designed to help you sort out the complex choices involved in moving data in the context of replication. These patterns were selected based on workshops and reviews with customers, partners, and industry luminaries, who identified this set as being of critical importance now.

Within this constrained view of data replication, the Pattern Frame organizes the collection of patterns into meaningful subcategories, such as how the data is organized, how it is used by applications, how it is deployed, and what sort of infrastructure it runs on. These subcategories can each be viewed from the perspectives of architecture, design, or implementation.

Pattlets

A pattlet describes a solution to a problem, but does not contain a detailed description of the context, problem, or forces that may impact the solution. Pattlets are required because elaborating on all patterns in the graph takes a significant amount of effort and time. Patterns need to evolve as the collective understanding of them evolves.

Deferring patterns until later, however, leaves holes in the pattern graph, which could result in related patterns suddenly becoming disconnected. To preserve the integrity of the relationships inside the pattern graph, this guide includes the patterns that were not included in the first release as *pattlets*. Pattlets are actual patterns that have not yet been documented in detail.

Summary

This chapter demonstrated how patterns provide a vocabulary to efficiently describe complex solutions without sacrificing detail. Effectively, the patterns form a new language with which architects and designers can communicate their thinking.

Because of the large number of patterns involved in building enterprise solutions, it can seem difficult to learn this new language. The guide structures the patterns into smaller, more closely related sets of patterns. This allows you to get started by using a smaller set of patterns, depending on your specific interest or the stage of the project.

In this chapter, four mechanisms have been introduced to help you navigate the patterns:

- **Relationships.** Relationships between patterns help you to identify patterns that are closely associated to the pattern you are using.
- **Clusters.** Clusters group patterns that belong to a common subject area
- **Levels of abstraction.** Levels of abstraction allow you to describe concepts in a manner that is consistent with the level of detail of your discussion.
- **Viewpoints.** Viewpoints help you select the vocabulary that is relevant to a team's particular role.

These mechanisms are not meant to constrain your thinking, but instead are intended to make looking at complex systems easier. With practice, you can naturally switch between these mechanisms as you switch between roles, subject areas, and levels of detail.

3

Data Movement Patterns

In the early days of enterprise data, data processing was highly centralized. Everything existed in mainframes and data was primarily operational. A single copy of a database or file was shared by many applications. The functions that data processing supported were also clearly divided: online work during the day and offline (batch) work at night.

Gradually functions blurred. Informational data began to be extracted from the operational data to provide analysis and reporting. More systems were added, including smaller departmental systems. Although certain databases (usually still at the center) were still designated as the systems of record, applications were increasingly being installed on distributed systems, first on midrange computers and then on personal computers. These distributed systems collected new data and required access to the central data as well. This drove the need for providing the systems with their own copies of data to work on. This also began to open the Pandora's box of distributed data problems, especially as metadata and then knowledge data were introduced. It also raised the core question for multiple copies of data. Do you manage the data integrity through distributed updates from the applications, or update the local copy of data only and then manage the copy integrity through data movement services?

The concept of data warehousing recognized the need to stop proliferating the number of point-to-point informational data extracts and find a more manageable and reusable approach. This led to the definition of Extract, Transform, and Load (ETL) services, which has become industry-standard terminology for a certain class of data movement services.

Recently, Relational Database Management Systems (RDBMSs) have started to offer facilities that make it easy to replicate data. This is a valuable addition, but questions remain about how replication and ETL differ, and how both of these differ from the previous concept of creating an extract.

The result of this evolution is that the problem of moving data copies has become extremely complex. This set of data movement patterns addresses a subset of the problems involved with maintaining copies of data. The pattern graph in Figure 3.1 shows the full set of patterns currently provided. These patterns were selected based on workshops and reviews with customers, partners, and industry luminaries, who identified this set as being of critical importance now.

The patterns start at a high-level abstract architectural viewpoint. They then elaborate through increasing levels of detail, down to detailed design patterns. Both the architecture and design-level patterns are independent of the technology that you will choose to implement the patterns. Product considerations are introduced only at the implementation level. The implementation patterns provide best-practices guidance for implementing the designs indicated by using Microsoft® SQL Server™.

Figure 3.1 shows the data movement pattern cluster in the patterns frame.

Notice that four pattlets are named, as well as twelve patterns. A *pattlet* is a placeholder for a pattern that is believed to exist, but that has not yet been written. It is important to be clear that this is not a comprehensive set of pattlets. These are merely the pattlets that are key to establishing the context for the Data Movement patterns. Many more pattlets could have been named, for example *Incremental Row-Level Replication*. These pattlets are omitted to avoid overburdening Figure 3.1 and to focus on delivering high quality in the set of patterns that our guiding customers and partners identified as key.

Also notice that this view of the Pattern Frame uses two kinds of lines: solid and dotted. Each line indicates either an inheritance relationship, where a pattern inherits concepts from a previous one, or a more relaxed relationship, which indicates that one pattern *can use* another. For example, *Master-Master Replication* can use *Master-Slave Snapshot Replication* for its initial setup. And *Master-Slave Replication* can use *Master-Slave Cascading Replication* as a deployment design.

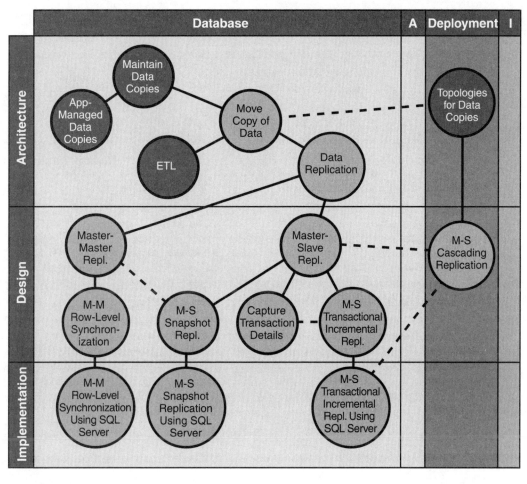

Figure 3.1
Data Movement patterns cluster

Architecture: Data Movement Root Patterns

Figure 3.2 shows the root patterns of Data Movement cluster, which address the issue of how to maintain the overall integrity of a set of data copies. These patterns presume that you already have or are about to have more than one copy of the same data in more than one place. They also assume that when an application makes a change to the original data, you want that change to be reflected in some other place. You might want to have the changes reflected within the same application unit of work; or you might want them to be reflected after that unit of work completes. You might also want the changes reflected as soon as possible or according to some other schedule.

Note: Making changes may include writing a copy of the change to an intermediary mechanism that the application recognises such as a user-created change log, or a messaging system. However, this is still within the application's local scope and changes will still be moved asynchronously.

The root pattlet, *Maintain Data Copies*, sets the context for the overall patterns cluster, which is that you want to create more than one copy of the same data. Your problem is how to serve the applications that will use all the copies and maintain the required state of integrity between the copies. The general solution is either to write synchronously to the copies from the originating transaction, or to post data synchronously to a local cache for later movement by an asynchronous service. The timeliness is given by the requirements of the applications.

The *Application-Managed Data Copies* pattlet shows that there is a cluster of patterns in the topic that are not yet addressed. These patterns would address the situation where the application ensures that copies of the data or derived data are updated during the same transaction which changed the original data.

The *Move Copy of Data* pattern is the root of the Data Movement patterns cluster. This architectural pattern is the root pattern for any type of asynchronous writing of copies of data. The pattern presents the fundamental data movement building block consisting of source, data movement link, and target. The data movement link consists of Acquire, Manipulate, and Write services. Transmissions in such a data movement building block are done asynchronously some time after the source is updated. Thus, the target applications must tolerate a certain amount of latency until changes are delivered. The rest of the Data Movement patterns follow from this pattern.

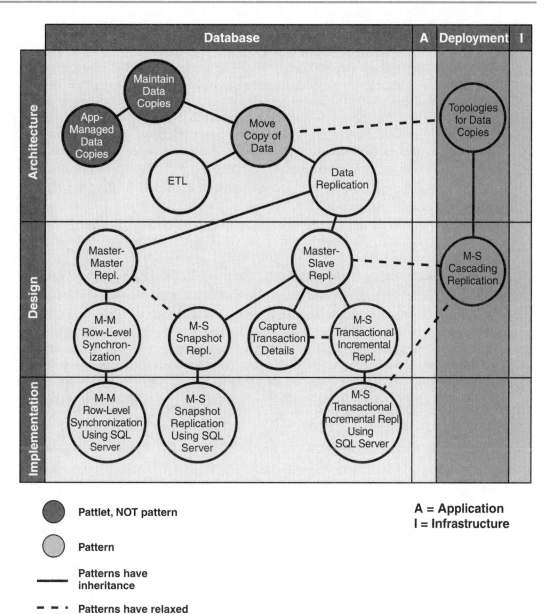

Figure 3.2
Root patterns for the Data Movement cluster

Architecture: Move Copy of Data Approaches

The *Move Copy of Data* pattern just introduced identifies and distinguishes between two key architectural approaches to moving copies: *ETL* and *Data Replication*. Both of these approaches refine the architectural approach described in *Move Copy of Data*. The difference between them is in the complexity of the Acquire, Manipulate, and Write services described in the data movement building block. Figure 3.3 highlights the pattern and pattlet representing these two approaches to moving copies.

Data Replication applies the data movement building block to solve problems where the data copies involved are basically identical. The *Acquire* service gets the replication set from the source. Acquiring the data is straightforward and requires almost no manipulation before sending it on to the copies. The writing of the data (performed by the Write service) may also be simple, but if there are complexities they occur in the write stage. The complexities often arise due to the common data in the copies being updatable at any of the copies, and the consequent need to update conflicts across the copies.

ETL takes its name from the industry standard term Extract, Transform, and Load. This pattern applies when acquiring the data for copying is very complex due to the number and technical variety of the data stores involved. The Acquire service is therefore called Extract to distinguish it from the simple Acquire used in *Data Replication*. The pattern also applies when the data requires complex manipulation, such as aggregation, cleansing, and related-data lookup for enrichment, before it can be sent on to the copy. This complex form manipulation is called Transform to distinguish it from the simple Manipulate service described in *Data Replication*. Writing the data (called Load to distinguish it from the Write service described in *Data Replication*) is simple, because only one copy of the data is ever updatable, and typically the copies are simply overwritten with new data. *ETL* is commonly used to provision a data warehouse which has a radically different schema to the operational databases that provide it with data, and to clean up and clarify the data for users before it is put into the warehouse.

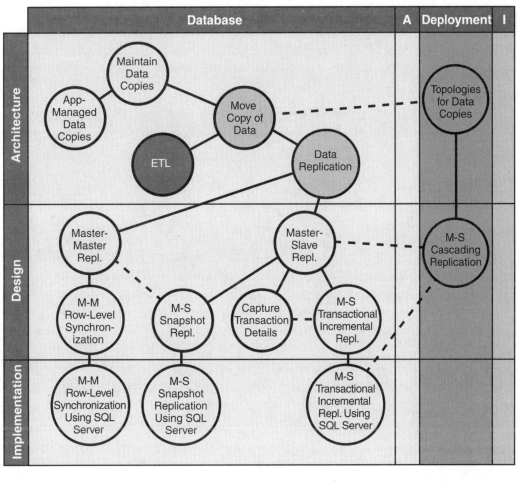

Figure 3.3
Move Copy of Data root

Design and Implementation: Data Replication Patterns

The remainder of the Data Movement cluster focuses on refining *Data Replication* through various design and implementation patterns, which are highlighted in Figure 3.4.

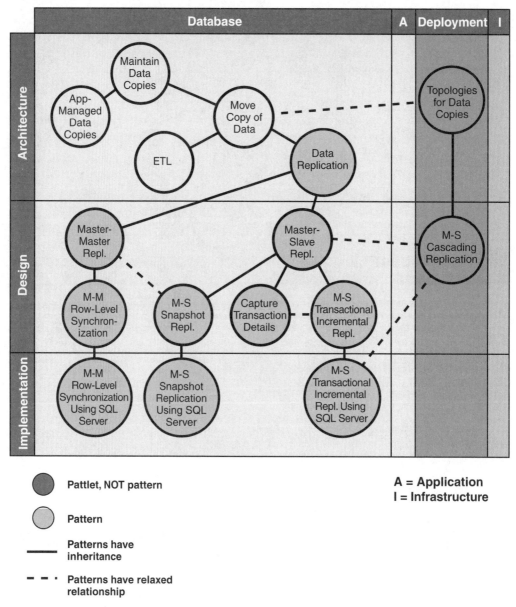

Figure 3.4
Data Replication patterns

The first key distinction, when refining *Data Replication*, is whether the replication is a *master-master* or *master-slave* type of replication.

The *Master-Master Replication* pattern describes the situation in which the same data can be updated in more than one copy (including the original); this creates the potential for different versions of the same data to exist. Any conflicts must be detected when the next replication occurs, and the conflicts have to be resolved according to some set of defined rules to maintain integrity. A common scenario here is when laptops work offline and make data changes, then need to synchronize the data changes with a shared server database which has been updated by other applications in the meantime.

Note: Do not confuse the term *master* with the term *prime*. *Master* means that the copied data is updateable in that location, and that those changes must persist locally and must be replicated to some other copy. *Prime* means that this is the originating source of the data, which provides the system of record for the particular instance of the data. If you want to know the true state of the data, in a business sense, at any point in time, you go to the prime copy. It is possible for data to have the attributes of both prime and master; however, these terms describe different aspects of the data relationships.

The *Master-Slave Replication* pattern describes a one-way flow of data from the master to the slave copy or copies. In addition, the master data is seen as having priority over the other copies; that is, if any changes have been made to any of the slave copies since the last replication, these can be overwritten by the next replication from the master to the slaves. However, there are cases in which slave changes persist after a replication: for example when replication only adds to the slave data, rather than updating or replacing it.

An additional design pattern that takes context from *Master-Master Replication* is *Master-Master Row-Level Synchronization*. This pattern synchronizes a pair of master-master copies that have common data that is updatable at either copy. It describes how to detect and resolve conflicts at a row level. The second of the master copies must be created in a state that is consistent with the original master copy. You can use *Master-Slave Snapshot Replication* for this one-time need. This "can use" relationship is indicated by the dotted line in the Pattern Frame (see Figure 3.4). *Master-Master Row-Level Synchronization Using SQL Server* shows how to implement the *Master-Master Row-Level Synchronization* design pattern by using SQL Server.

The other design and implementation patterns take context from *Master-Slave Replication*. *Master-Slave Snapshot Replication* is a pattern for creating a point-in-time copy of defined data. The copy consists of the entire set of data that is to be replicated, not just the changes since the last replication. The *Capture Transaction Details* pattern shows how to capture application changes made to the master data when either you do not have a DBMS-provided transaction log or you do not want to use that log for some reason. The result is a cache of data changes that can be used by *Master-Slave Transactional Incremental Replication*. This is a pattern for solving how to update copies by sending only the transactional data changes that have occurred in the master to the slave copies (rather than using the entire set of all row information). The pattern ensures that replicated data is available to applications only after dependent operations of the same transaction have been replicated.

As their names suggest, *Implementing Master-Slave Snapshot Replication Using SQL Server* and *Implementing Master-Slave Transactional Incremental Replication Using SQL Server* show SQL Server implementations of the respective design patterns.

Data Replication Deployment

The patterns highlighted in Figure 3.5 (on the next page) provide deployment guidance for *Data Replication*.

Currently, only a pattlet is provided at the architecture level. *Topologies for Data Copies* indicates that deploying a complex topology for moving redundant data involves a multistep use of the data movement building block described in *Move Copy of Data*.

The *Master-Slave Cascading Replication* pattern describes how to replicate data from one copy to many other copies, all of which require the same data. Figure 3.5 indicates that this deployment pattern is suitable for master-slave deployments only (not for master-master deployments). It also indicates that you can use *Implementing Master-Slave Transactional Incremental Replication Using SQL Server* to implement the *Master-Slave Cascading Replication* pattern.

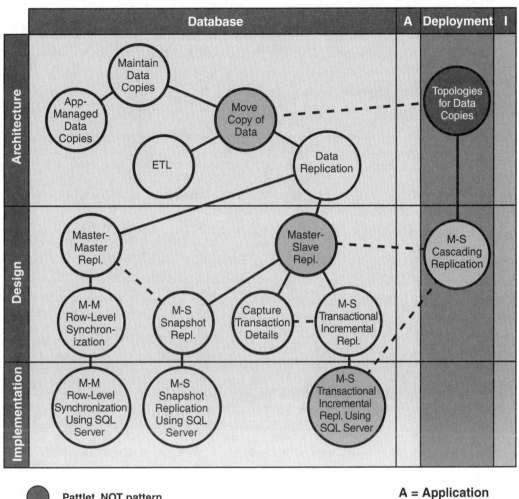

Figure 3.5
Data Replication Deployment patterns

Data Movement Patterns

The following table lists all of the patterns and pattlets identified in the Data Movement patterns cluster.

Table 3.1: Data Movement Patterns Cluster

Pattern or Pattlet Name	Problem Description	Solution Description
Maintain Data Copies (pattlet)	What proven architectural approach should you follow to maintain the content of data that exists in more than one place?	This root pattlet sets the context for the pattern cluster overall. The context is that you have, or are about to create, more than one copy of some data. The general solution is to either synchronously write to the copies from the originating application, or to synchronously post data to a local cache for later movement by an asynchronous service. The timeliness of that movement is given by the requirements of the applications.
Application-Managed Data Copies (pattlet)	What proven architectural approach should you follow to design synchronous data management services when you have data held in more than one data stores that are serving applications?	In this case, when a particular application makes a change to its copy of the data, it should then also make changes to the other copies. The application ensures that copies of the data and/or derived data are updated in the same transaction that changed the original data.
Move Copy of Data	What proven architectural approach should you follow to design data movement services when you have data held in data stores that are serving applications, and now you want other applications to use copies of that data?	This is the root pattern for any type of asynchronous writing of copies of data. The pattern presents the fundamental data movement building block, which consists of source, data movement set, data movement link, and target. Transmissions in such a data movement building block are done asynchronously (or eventually) after the update of the source. Thus, the target applications must tolerate certain latency until changes are delivered.

Pattern or Pattlet Name	Problem Description	Solution Description
Data Replication	What proven architectural approach should you follow to create nearly-identical copies of the data, and possibly also allow the copies to be updated at either the source or target with changes being reflected in each other?	This pattern presents a special type of data movement (replication) with a simple acquisition and manipulation of the data, but possibly a complex write. The complexity of the write generally arises from the need to update both source and target and to eventually exchange the changes to the counterpart.
Extract-Transform-Load (ETL) (pattlet)	What proven architectural approach should you follow to create copies of the data when data flows one-way to the target, but getting the data is complex and it needs to be changed a lot before it can be written to the target?	ETL is a type of data movement with possibly a complex acquisition from heterogeneous sources, and/or a complex manipulation with aggregation and cleansing, but always a simple write by overwriting any changes on the target
Master-Master Replication	How do you design a replication where the replication set is updateable at either end, the changes need to be transmitted to the other party, and any conflicts need to be detected and resolved?	This is bidirectional data replication between source and target. This includes conflict detection and resolution in order to handle concurrent updates to different copies of the same data in the same transmission interval.
Master-Slave Replication	How do you design replication when the copy is read-only, or it may be updated but changes to the copied data are not transmitted back, and they may be overwritten on a later replication transmission?	This is unidirectional data replication from a source to a target, with overwrite of the target data by the transmission.
Master-Master Row-Level Synchronization	How do you design a replication to transmit data from the source to the target and vice versa, when the same replication set is updateable on both sides and you want to resolve conflicts at the row level?	A specific master-master replication where conflict detection and resolution are done at a row level.

(continued)

Pattern or Pattlet Name	Problem Description	Solution Description
Master-Slave Snapshot Replication	How do you design a master-slave replication to copy the entire replication set so that it is consistent at a given point in time?	A specific master-slave replication where the complete replication set is acquired from the source, possibly manipulated and written to the target. This design is also used for incremental replications and synchronizations to create the first copy of the data to be maintained.
Capture Transaction Details	How do you design a recording of transactional information for all changes to a data store so you can use these as a source for replication?	Design of recording transactional information by means of handcrafted artifacts to be used in an incremental replication using transactional changes. Required if there is no database management system (DBMS) transaction log or if the transaction log cannot be used for any reasons.
Master-Slave Transactional Incremental Replication	How do you design a replication link to support the transmission of changes using transactional details and replaying them on the target while meeting all integrity constraints?	A specific master-slave replication that transmits transactional information from the source and applies it to the target. This ensures that changed data is available to applications only after dependent operations of the same transaction have been replicated as well.
Implementing Master-Master Row-Level Synchronization Using SQL Server	How do you implement this design using Microsoft SQL Server?	Guidance to implement synchronization with row-level conflict detection and resolution by means provided with SQL Server merge replication.
Implementing Master-Slave Snapshot Replication Using SQL Server	How do you implement this design using SQL Server?	Guidance to implement snapshot replication by means provided with SQL Server snapshot replication.
Implementing Master-Slave Transactional Incremental Replication Using SQL Server	How do you implement this design using SQL Server?	Guidance to implement incremental replication using transactional information by means provided with with SQL Server transactional replication.

Pattern or Pattlet Name	Problem Description	Solution Description
Topologies for Data Copies (pattlet)	What are the proven architectural approaches for creating a topology of data copies for deployments?	The architectural approaches to deploying data copies on several platforms.
Master-Slave Cascading Replication	How can you optimize the replication of a set of targets in a master-slave environment, and minimize the impact on the source?	A deployment design for master-slave replications, where the replication from a single source to several targets uses a concatenation of replication links with intermediary databases serving both as target and source. The copies are all related by a need for data from the source replication set.

Move Copy of Data

Context

You have data held in data stores that are serving applications and now you want other applications to use that data. You have decided that:

- You do not want the other applications to access the source data.
- You want to provide these other applications with a redundant copy of the data. In other words, you want to move a copy of the data to the other applications.

The structure of the data required by the other applications may be exactly the same as that of the existing data or it may be completely different.

Note: The term *data store* refers to a collection of data that is managed by a database management system (DBMS) or is held in a file system.

Problem

What proven architectural approach should you follow to design the data movement services?

Forces

Any of the following **compelling forces** would justify using the solution described in this pattern:

- **Data availability no longer matches requirements.** For example, your existing centralized data stores were designed to support regular business hours of 08:00 to 18:00, and these data stores must be taken offline for after-hours maintenance and reporting. Your other applications, however, must support customer-direct self-service, which requires 24-hour availability. Another example is you are writing applications that are going to be installed on laptops for a mobile field force that requires the data to be available while working offline. This requires copying the data to the laptops and synchronizing changes later when the laptops reconnect to the network.

- **Network or application platform is unreliable.** For example, your network fails frequently or is shut down for significant periods of time so that your new applications cannot deliver the required levels of service.

- **Your other applications require differently structured data.** The existing data store uses a structure that is suitable for the existing applications. If the other applications, however, require the data to be stored in a different structure, you may have to store the data redundantly in both structures.

- **Network bandwidth does not support real-time data access performance requirements.** In this case you may need to avoid the real-time problem by making a local data copy available.

Hint: This force can lead to disaster if you misjudge it. Your early requirements, benchmarks, or prototyping might lead you to believe that the bandwidth is acceptable. However, a new or rapidly growing application can degrade performance quickly. The redundant data approach can minimize the effects of these changes. This approach carries its own risk, though, if the volume of data to be copied increases significantly, if latency requirements change, or if network bandwidth drops at the time you need to copy the data.

The following **enabling forces** facilitate the adoption of the solution, and their absence may hinder such a move:

- **Latency tolerance.** The other applications must be able to tolerate the wait that is associated with moving the data.
- **Data changes are generally non-conflicting.** Often the business use of the data makes it relatively easy to isolate changes to the original data and its copies. For example, if you are providing a new application on a laptop for a client manager to use when making customer calls, the manager may update client data during the call. It is highly unlikely that the customer will call the company and request changes to an existing copy of the data during the same time period.
- **Other applications require only read access or do not require updates to the target to persist.** In these circumstances, the process of providing these applications with a copy of data to use locally can be much simpler, and hence easier to implement. Do not assume, however, that because providing a copy is simpler in these circumstances, it is the best solution.

Solution

Create a basic architectural building block and use it alone, or in combination with other such blocks to assemble a solution of greater complexity. The basic architectural building block is called a *data movement building block*.

The data movement building block consists of the following items:

- A movement set in a source data store
- A data movement link that provides a path from source to target and contains the Acquire, Manipulate, and Write services
- A target data store

Figure 3.6 on the next page illustrates a data movement building block.

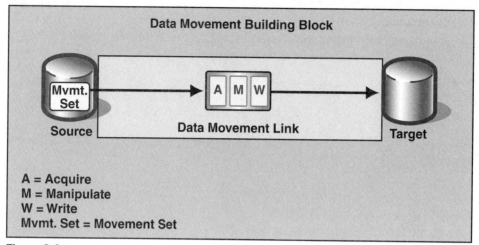

Figure 3.6
Data movement building block

In the figure, the arrows represent the directional flow of the movement set. This does not mean that these are the only data actions. For example, in other data patterns, the Write service gets data from the target.

Source

The *source* is a data store that contains a set of data to be copied. One data store can be the source for many data movement building blocks. The source data store can also serve as the target for another data movement building block. For example, in the *Master-Master Replication* pattern, the same pair of data stores swap roles (source becomes target, and target becomes source) for a common movement set that can be updated in either data store.

Movement Set

A *movement set* is an identified subset of data that is copied from a single source and sent across a data movement link to one or more targets. In the course of the copy operation, the movement set may change its content and form as it is acquired, manipulated, and written. For example, if you want to copy data from a server to laptops for salespersons to use in making daily calls, each person needs a movement set containing the details of the clients that they are going to call on that day. Thus a movement set is the name for the subject of a data copy operation at all stages of that operation. In the course of the copy operation, the movement set may change its content and form as it is acquired, manipulated, and written.

Variant: Composite Movement Set

An application may require redundant data from more than one existing database. A *composite movement set* comprises all the data you intend to replicate for any particular application. The application's requirements are what binds this grouping of data together and gives it a purpose.

Figure 3.7 illustrates a composite movement set composed of data from two sources.

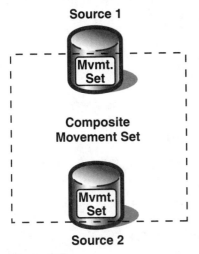

Figure 3.7
Composite movement set

As the figure shows, a composite movement set is a collection of one or more movement sets. For example, the application on your salesperson's laptop needs client data, which might all come from Source 1. The application, however, also needs the contract data related to the clients from Source 2. Each movement set is part of a data movement building block. Both movement sets must be acquired together to select those contracts that are related to the clients.

Data Movement Link

A *data movement link* is a connection between the source and target along which the relevant movement set can be moved from one data store to another with appropriate security. Moving this data across the link is called a *transmission*.

The data movement link includes:

- The method of data transmission at each step that moves data (which includes any intermediary transient data stores). For example, the transmission method might be shared data storage, FTP, or a secure electronic link with managed row transmission.

- The Acquire, Manipulate, and Write data movement services.

Acquire

The *Acquire* service gets the movement set from the source data store. Acquisition may be a simple one-step process, or it may be a multi-step process, for example if the movement set is in several tables in the data store.

Acquire may enrich the data by adding details, such as the time the data was acquired, to allow for management of the overall data integrity.

Acquire can obtain the movement sets from the data store rows directly, or it may acquire them from data caches where only data changes are stored. Typically these are either DBMS log record stores or user-written caching data stores. In this case, these stores should be considered the sources.

When acquiring data from these stores, Acquire must either collect all transactional changes or collect the net change, which is the final result of all changes that have occurred to this row since the last transmission.

Hint: If Acquire collects all transactional changes, the ordering of the changes is vital so that the Write service can follow the correct change sequence. This correct order can be difficult to establish across a composite movement set being acquired through multiple data movement building blocks. You may decide to acquire the composite movement set from one Acquire service so you can order the set. Even then you may have problems with time-clock inconsistencies across platforms. On the other hand, if Acquire collects the net change instead, you have to define rules to resolve the conflicts that arise (for an example, see the *Master-Master Row-Level Synchronization* pattern).

Manipulate

The *Manipulate* service changes the form of the data in some way and passes it on in a format that can easily be written to the target. Manipulate can vary in complexity from a null event (where it does nothing to change the data) to very radical data alternations. More detailed architectural patterns discuss this topic.

Write

The *Write* service writes the data that Manipulate prepared to the target. If Write finds that the target has changed the data that it got from the last data movement, then Write must conform to the attributes on the data movement link regarding how to behave; it must either force the new data over the target data, write the new data somewhere else, and raise an error, or it must take some conflict resolution action. These issues are discussed in the replication design patterns.

Target

In a data movement building block, the target is the data store where the acquired and manipulated data is written. As noted earlier, sometimes the target can be several data stores.

If the data that you move to the target can be updated by applications there, and if the changes must be reflected back into the source, you should have a second data movement link returning so that the roles of source and target are exchanged on this link. This relationship must be explicit because of the data integrity issues; it is a data movement link attribute and is described in the *Master-Master Replication* pattern.

Resulting Context

This pattern results in the following benefits and liabilities:

Benefits

- **Target data store optimization.** The Target data stores can be configured and optimized in different ways to best support their different types of data access. For example, one case might be about manipulating individual rows, while another might be about reports on many records.

- **Data autonomy.** When the data stores are relatively independent of each other and can have different owners, the content of the source data store can be provided as a product, and it is then the responsibility of the target owner to operate on its data.

- **Data privacy.** By restricting the movement set to an agreed subset of the source data store, *Move Copy of Data* can provide only data that the application (or users) at the target may see.

- **Security.** Source data stores are not accessed by the target applications and hence are more secure.

Liabilities

- **Administration complexity.** This pattern may introduce additional operational tasks for data store administrators. For example, the ongoing transmissions have to be checked to ensure that they are running smoothly. Also, administrators must monitor the impact of the involved resources, such as the growth of cached changes, log files, and so on.

- **Potential increased overhead on the sources.** Every acquisition of data loads a certain overhead on the source. It is important to properly plan the additional load caused by extracting snapshots or by logging transactions that will replicated. The additional load has to be compared to the load that would occur if all applications were connected to a single data store. You can use this pattern to optimize the operational load.

- **Potential security exposure.** The target data stores must not allow access to source data that the source would not permit. This is another administration challenge.

Next Considerations

After you have decided to implement the data movement solution, the next challenge is to decide between the *Data Replication* and *Extract-Transform-Load (ETL)* patterns. The distinguishing criterion is the complexity of the data movement link, which essentially translates to one of the following options:

- *ETL* **is appropriate if Acquire and Manipulate are complex, but Write is relatively simple.** An ETL process can handle complex acquisition, such as merging data from heterogeneous sources. ETL also allows for complex manipulations, such as cleansing of the acquired data or aggregations.

- *Replication* **is appropriate if Acquire and Manipulate are simple, and Write is also either simple or it is complex because of conflict detection and resolution.** A replication process generally reads a single source only and the manipulations are restricted to calculations on a current record, such as data type conversions, concatenating, or splitting strings. Write can detect changes in the target that have occurred since the last transmission and resolve any resulting conflicts by defined rules.

Examples

The following examples illustrate how to use the data movement building block to solve common data movement problems of differing complexity. Some of these examples reappear in later patterns in this cluster.

Simple Data Movement for Reporting Purposes

The simplest use of this pattern moves data to a data mart or warehouse when the schema of the mart or warehouse is very similar to the counterparts in the operational data store. In this example, you need to build a new system that provides online transaction processing (OLTP) transactions and summarized reports based on the information of the previous day. The summary reports are not updatable; they are management reports and are not used for what-if analysis. You do not want the platform that hosts the operational data store to bear the additional load of the reporting and the additional complexity for accessing the previous day's data.

The solution is to implement a data movement link with target overwrite between the operational source data store and a reporting target data store as shown in Figure 3.8. (In this data movement, the applications on the target data store are either read-only or any updates to the movement set are not to be moved back to the source data store.)

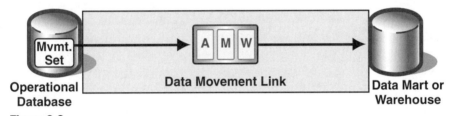

Figure 3.8
Simple data movement from an operational data store to an informational data store

The operational data store remains available for the ongoing transactions. Every night a snapshot from the operational data store is taken and transferred to the reporting data store. Because all elements of the data movement link are simple, the implementation can follow the *Data Replication* pattern.

Complex Data Movement for Reporting Purposes

Frequently, the mart and warehouse schemas are very different, or the manipulation is very complex.

Suppose you have three source data stores, two of which are independent databases and one of which is a flat file. You plan to merge the contents of the data stores, which have partially overlapping information. Analysis shows that the data acquired from the different data stores contains some contradictions. Thus, you must do some data cleansing in the movement process. In addition, the target does not present the information on the same detailed level as the source, but it does aggregate the raw data and write these summaries to the target only.

The solution is to apply the *ETL* pattern because the Write is still simple. Figure 3.9 on the next page shows a sketch of the solution with the complex parts highlighted.

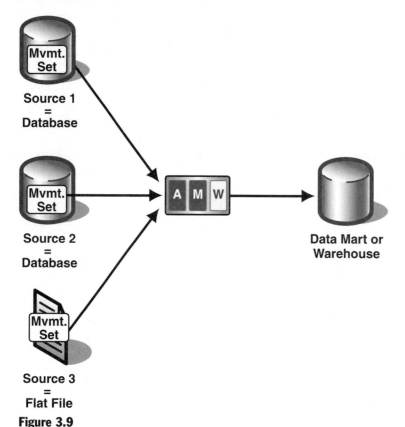

Figure 3.9
Complex data movement from several data stores to an informational data store

Master-Master Data Movement

In a master-master data movement, any changes that the target makes to the copied data are sent back to the source so that the source can stay synchronized with the target. Figure 3.10 illustrates this type of data movement.

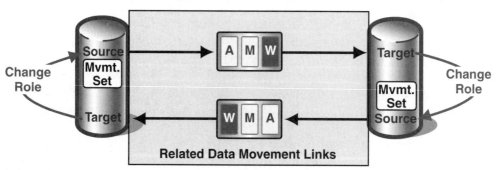

Figure 3.10
Master-master data movement

This particular source-target relationship is two-way, and this is implemented by a pair of related data movement links. Write must include logic for conflict detection and conflict resolution. That is, it must check to see if the data has changed since the last transmission. If so, any conflicts must be resolved according to defined rules.

The solution is to apply *Data Replication* because Acquire and Manipulate are simple, but Write is complex. Then use the *Master-Master Replication* pattern, which deals with the conflict detection and resolution issues.

Related Patterns

For more information, see the following related patterns:

Patterns That May Have Led You Here

- *Maintain Data Copies.* This pattern may have led you to *Move Copy of Data*, based on your requirements and the complexity of your environment.

Patterns That You Can Use Next

- *Data Replication.* As mentioned in "Resulting Context," *Move Copy of Data* leads naturally to *Data Replication*, depending on the level of complexity of the data movement link. *Data Replication* presents the architecture of a data movement, where Acquire and Manipulate are relatively simple, but Write might be complex.
- *Extract-Transform-Load (ETL).* As mentioned in "Resulting Context," *Move Copy of Data* leads naturally to *ETL*, depending on the level of complexity of the data movement link. *ETL* describes the architecture of a data movement, where Acquire and Manipulate may by complex, but Write is always simple.

Other Patterns of Interest

- *Publisher-Subscriber.* The data movement building block is an instance of the more general *Publisher-Subscriber* pattern where a publisher offers a content publication service and subscribers subscribe to all or parts of the publication service.

Data Replication

Context

You have decided to follow the *Move Copy of Data* pattern. Furthermore:

- You want to move data between two identical or very nearly identical data stores.
- You may have to allow the data involved to be updated by applications at either the source or the target, and if so you must manage the integrity of those changes.

Note: For simplicity, this pattern describes replicating between relational databases. The concepts, however, apply to other types of data stores as well.

Problem

What proven architectural approach should you follow to create nearly-identical copies of the data and to manage the integrity of the copies if they can be updated at both the source and target within a replication interval?

Forces

Most of the forces that were described in the *Move Copy of Data* pattern apply in this context and there are no additional ones. The relevant forces are repeated here for convenience.

Any of the following **compelling forces** would justify using the solution described in this pattern:

- **Data availability no longer matches requirements.** For example, your existing centralized data stores were designed to support regular business hours of 08:00 to 18:00, and these data stores must be taken offline for after-hours maintenance and reporting. Your other applications, however, must support customer-direct self-service, which requires 24-hour availability. Another example is you are writing applications that are going to be installed on laptops for a mobile field force that require the data to be available while working offline. This requires copying the data to the laptops and synchronizing changes later when the laptops reconnect to the network.

- **Network or application platform is unreliable.** For example, your network fails frequently or is shut down for significant periods of time so that your new applications cannot deliver the required levels of service.

- **Network bandwidth does not support real-time data access performance requirements.** In this case, you might need to avoid the real-time problem by making a local data copy available.

Hint: This force can lead to disaster if you misjudge it. Your early requirements, benchmarks, or prototyping might lead you to believe that the bandwidth is acceptable. However, a new or rapidly growing application can degrade performance quickly. The redundant data approach can minimize the effects of these changes. This approach carries its own risk, though, if the volume of data to be copied increases significantly, if latency requirements change, or if network bandwidth drops at the time you need to copy the data.

The following **enabling forces** facilitate the move to the solution, and their absence may hinder such a move:

- **Latency tolerance.** The other applications must be able to tolerate the wait that is associated with moving the data.

- **Data changes are generally non-conflicting.** Often the business use of the data makes it relatively easy to isolate changes to the original data and its copies. For example, if you are providing a new application on a laptop for a client manager to use when making customer calls, the manager may update client data during the call. It is highly unlikely that the customer will call the company and request changes to an existing copy of the data during the same time period.

Solution

Build on the data movement building block as described in *Move Copy of Data* by adding refinements that are appropriate to replication. To focus the terminology, the base building block for this pattern is called a *replication building block*. Also, in the special circumstances of the *Master-Master Replication* pattern, the building block will have a pair of related replication links to handle the two-way nature of the replication.

For the same reason, the data movement link is called *replication link;* the replication link transmits a *replication set* across the link. In the link, the Acquire and Write services are always simple, and the Write service may be simple (as in the *Master-Slave Replication* pattern) or complex (as in the *Master-Master Replication* pattern).

Figure 3.11 on the next page illustrates a replication building block.

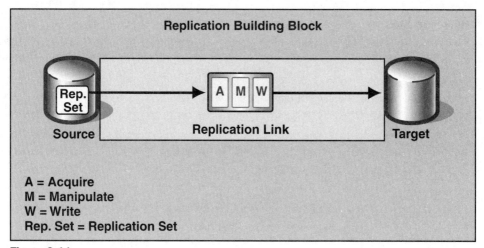

Figure 3.11
Replication building block

The following paragraphs describe the elements of the replication building block in comparison to the more generic elements of the data movement building block.

Source

In a replication building block, the source is generally a database that contains data to be replicated. One database can be the source for many replication building blocks. The source database can also serve as the target for another replication building block. For example, in the *Master-Master Replication* pattern, the same pair of data stores swap roles (source becomes target, and target becomes source) for a common movement set that is updateable in either data store.

Replication Set

A *replication set* is an identified set of data that exists within a single source, and it corresponds to the movement set. It is the subset of the particular database that you want to acquire for replication. For example, if you want to replicate data to a laptop for salespersons to use in making daily calls, each person needs a replication set containing the details of the clients that they are going to call on that day.

A replication set is made up of a group of replication units. A *replication unit* is the smallest amount of data that can be identified in a transmission. The replication unit can be any one of the following:

- The complete replication set
- A table of the replication set
- A transaction
- A row (from a table of the replication set)
- A column (from a row of a table of the replication set)

Replication Link

The replication link corresponds to the data movement link with specific refinements for replication.

A *replication link* is a connection between the source and target along which the relevant data is replicated from one database to another with appropriate security. Movement of a replication set across the link is called a *transmission*.

The replication link includes:

- The method of transmission of data at each step that moves data (which includes any intermediary transient data stores). For example, the method of transmission may be shared data storage, FTP, or a secure electronic link with managed row transmission.

- The Acquire, Manipulate, and Write replication services.

Acquire

The *Acquire* service gets the replication set from the source. Acquisition may be a simple one-step process, or it may be a multi-step process, for example if the replication set is in several tables in the data store, which could be a multistep process to acquire a *composite movement set*.

Hint: The *Data Replication* pattern works when you are dealing with composite movement sets for a single platform, but when multiple database management systems (DBMSs) and/or operating systems are involved, you probably need to use the *Extract-Transform-Load (ETL)* pattern.

Acquire can enrich the data by adding details, such as the time the data was acquired, to allow for management of the overall data integrity.

Acquire can obtain the replication sets from the database rows directly, or it can acquire them from data caches where only data changes are stored. Typically these are either DBMS log record stores or user-written caching databases. In this case, these stores should be considered the sources.

When acquiring data from these stores, Acquire must either collect all transactional changes or collect the net change, which is the final result of all the changes that have occurred to this row since the last transmission.

Hint: When you want to acquire a composite movement set, and you need to decide whether to follow the pattern and have a replication building block for each source, or to write a variant of Acquire that gets the whole set. This is the classic reusable modular code versus monolithic code question. Both approaches are valid in certain circumstances. In general, you can:

1. Use the multiple replication building block approach as your default. It is the most flexible and reusable, but you must evaluate whether it is efficient enough.

2. Use a composite movement set when the target set has a simple aggregated view of the source data. For example, you want to assemble a single view of customer data, and to do that you need extra customer data from many product databases. In the banking industry, this view could show that this customer has a current account, a savings account, and two mortgages. In the target, this is held in a single aggregated record. In the source, these are all held in separate Product databases on the same platform. There is a common identifier for Customer in all the databases. Acquire then fetches the customer details from each database, and Manipulate stitches them together for Write to write to the target. (If the situation is any more complex than this, though, you are getting into *ETL*).

Manipulate

The *Manipulate* service changes the form of the data in a simple way and passes it on in a format that can easily be written to the target.

The essence of replication is that manipulation is simple and can be performed either within the database language (SQL) or by a simple tool provided usually by the DBMS vendor. Manipulate should not contain complex logic of the sort that would require you to write applications to implement it. The simplest manipulation is a mapping to the target structure by using the tool or SQL. This may include semantic changes such as mapping to a date data type. Other valid manipulations are:

- Splitting or combining data elements or rows
- Code page translations
- Elementary data integrity checks, such as type validation
- Aggregation functions that can be performed simply within the technology

---

Note: The Manipulate service differs from the Transform service of *ETL* in the complexity of the change it performs. Although this difference can be difficult to characterize precisely, the goal is to differentiate *Data Replication* from *ETL*, which is another pattern.

Write

The *Write* service writes the data that the Manipulate service prepared to the target. If the target has changed the replication data since the last replication transmission, the Write service must check its rules to see whether it must resolve conflicts or not.

If it does not have to resolve the conflicts, then it has to decide whether to:

- Overwrite the target with the new transmission data.
- Append the new transmission data, in which case Write must handle row versioning.

If it does have to resolve the conflicts, the *Master-Master Replication* pattern applies for conflict detection and resolution.

Target

In a replication building block, the *target* is the database where the data is written. The structure of the target is very similar or identical to the source. The target could be several databases.

If the data that you replicate to the target can be updated by applications there, and if the changes need to be reflected back into the source, you should have a second replication link returning so that the roles of source and target are exchanged. This relationship must be explicit because of the data integrity issues; it is a replication link attribute and is described in the *Master-Master Replication* and *Master-Master Row-Level Synchronization* patterns.

Examples

The following examples illustrate how to use the replication building block.

Feeding Management Information Reports

You need to build a new system that provides online transaction processing (OLTP) transactions and summarized management information reports based on the information of the previous day. The summary reports are not updatable; they are management reports and are not used for what-if analysis. There are many reports that constitute a significant workload. You do not want the platform that hosts the operational database to bear the additional load of the reporting, and the additional complexity of accessing the previous day's data.

The solution is to implement a master-slave replication link between the operational source database and a reporting target database. For more information, see the *Master-Slave Replication*, *Master-Slave Snapshot Replication* and Master-Slave Transactional Incremental Replication design patterns.

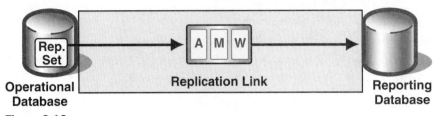

Figure 3.12
Replication from an operational database to a reporting database

Provisioning a Mobile Sales Force and Synchronizing Their Work

Sales forces must have product and customer information available during their visits. They want to update customer information such as addresses immediately.

The solution is to implement a *master-master replication* link between the central customer source database and the sales force laptop target databases. For more information, see the *Master-Master Replication* and *Master-Master Row-Level Synchronization* patterns.

In a master-master replication, any changes that the target makes to the replicated data are sent back to the source, so that the source can stay synchronized with the target. Figure 3.13 illustrates this type of replication.

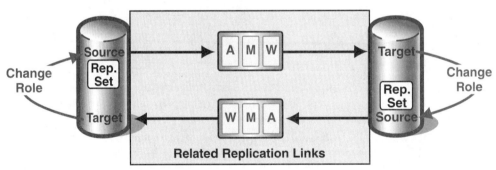

Figure 3.13
Master-master replication

Every sales representative gets an extract of an operational source database on his or her laptop. This target database can be updated while the laptop is disconnected from the master database. The next time the laptop is connected to the central database, any changes to the laptop target customer data are sent to the operational source database.

Provisioning a Large Number of Targets

Airline companies need a high volume of data for the computation of optimal flight routes for every individual flight. The data consists of weather information, fuel prices, flight rights on territories, and other restrictions. The data is only partially accessible in a machine-readable manner. One airline offers the service of maintaining this data in a database and provides the data to customers as a product. The customers can update the received data, but these updates are not sent back.

The solution is to implement the *Master-Slave Cascading Replication* pattern to provide the data to a large number of targets. For more information, see the *Master-Slave Replication* and *Master-Slave Cascading Replication* patterns.

The airline uses a central source database for data maintenance. From there, the data is replicated to an intermediary target database, which in turn serves as the source for replication to the customer sites. The replication is invoked immediately after every transaction.

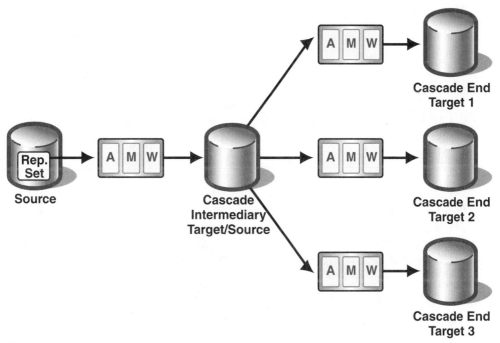

Figure 3.14
Cascading replication

Resulting Context

This pattern results in the same benefits and liabilities described in the *Move Copy of Data* pattern:

Benefits

- **Target data store optimization.** The Target data stores can be configured and optimized in different ways to best support their different types of data access. For example, one case might be about manipulating individual rows, while another might be about reports on many records.

- **Data autonomy.** When the data stores are relatively independent of each other and can have different owners, the content of the source data store can be provided as a product, and it is then the responsibility of the target owner to operate on its data.

- **Data privacy.** By restricting the movement set to an agreed subset of the source data store, *Move Copy of Data* can provide only data that the application (or users) at the target can see.

- **Security.** Source data stores are not accessed by the target applications and hence are more secure.

Liabilities

- **Administration complexity.** This pattern might introduce additional operational tasks for data store administrators. For example, the ongoing transmissions have to be checked to ensure that they are running smoothly. Also, administrators must monitor the impact of the involved resources, such as the growth of cached changes, log files, and so on.

- **Potential increased overhead on the sources.** Every acquisition of data loads a certain overhead on the source. It is important to properly plan the additional load caused by extracting snapshots or by logging transactions that will be replicated. The additional load has to be compared to the load that would occur if all applications were connected to a single data store. You can use this pattern to optimize the operational load.

- **Potential security exposure.** The target data stores must not allow access to source data that the source would not permit. This is another administration challenge.

Next Considerations

Use the pattern to build your own solution by following this simple process:

1. Analyze the other application's data requirements to identify the existing source databases that the solution will use.

2. Within these source databases, identify the actual data required by the other applications and map this set of tables/columns to the target.

3. Define the operational requirements for the target and match these requirements to the source capabilities to deliver the data.

4. Define the functional requirements on Acquire, Manipulate, and Write (AMW) for each replication building block, and hence design the end-to-end AMW process.

5. Determine how many replication building blocks your architecture will require by considering the overall topology that is required to deliver the operational requirements for both source and target. Hence, divide the AMW functions amongst these building blocks.

6. Define the replication links between databases, their attributes, and their relationships and hence plan the full replication deployment that meets the combined functional and operational requirements.

7. Understand the operational considerations for each of replication link, match them to the overall replication operational requirements, and thus create the schedule for each replication link.

To apply this process, you must consider the following design issues:

- **Replication set size.** Decide whether to replicate an entire table, a subset of a table, or data from more than one table. This is a tradeoff among the amount of data that changes, the overall table size, and the complexity of the link.

- **Transmission volume.** Choose the right amount of data to transmit. The decision between sending all changes for any one row, or just the net effect of all the changes, is a key one.

- **Replication set data changes at the target.** If these have to occur and if the source wants to see the changes, then try to make the changes naturally non-conflicting to avoid the need for conflict detection and resolution.

- **Replication frequency.** Decide the appropriate timing of the replication for the requirements and optimize the use of computing resources.

- **Replication unit.** As defined earlier, a replication set consists of a group of replication units. Identify the unit of data that will be transmitted from the source to the target. In the extreme requirements, this will be a transaction as it has been executed on the source. A less precise but easier to achieve requirement is to move a changed row. For environments with a high risk of conflicts, it can also be an individual change in a cell within a record.

- **Initiator.** Decide whether the source pushes the data or the target pulls it, and make sure that throughout your replication topology these decisions do not cause later replication links to have problems meeting their operational requirements.

- **Locking issues.** Verify that you can accept the locking impact of the replication on the source. If not, verify that a slight decrease in consistency at a point in time is acceptable for the targets so you can avoid lock conflict.

- **Replication topology.** Identify the players, their roles, and the overall integrity.

- **Security.** Ensure that the replicated data is treated with the right level of security at the target given the source security conditions. Also, verify that your replication link is secure enough in the overall topology requirements.

- **Key updates.** Verify whether the source allows updates to the key of records belonging to the replication set. If so, special care must be taken for a consistent replication of such operations.

Note: *Key updates* are SQL updates to the columns of the physical key within a replication set. Such key updates must be handled specially by the replication.

- **Referential integrity.** Verify whether the target has implemented referential integrity. If so, you need rules to prevent changes from the replication link being applied twice if the change triggers a target change in another replicated table.

Related Patterns

For more information, see the following related patterns:

Patterns That May Have Led You Here

- *Move Copy of Data.* The *Move Copy of Data* pattern describes the fundamental architecture building block from which *Data Replication* inherits basic concepts.

Patterns That You Can Use Next

- *Master-Master Replication.* This pattern discusses a situation in which changes occur to a common set of data at either source or target, and the other party wants such changes replicated to it.

- *Master-Slave Replication.* This pattern presents the solution for a replication where the changes are replicated to the target without taking changes of the target into account. It will eventually overwrite any changes on the target.

Other Patterns of Interest

- *Master-Slave Cascading Replication.* This pattern discusses a replication deployment where many targets want to subscribe to the replication set that is being replicated

- *Extract-Transform-Load (ETL).* This pattern is an alternative to *Data Replication*, if the Acquire or the Manipulate service is complex, but the Write service is simple.

Master-Master Replication

Context

You are about to design a replication between a source and a target. Your requirements are:

- Replication set is updateable at either end.
- Updates need to be transmitted to the other party.
- Conflicts need to be detected and resolved.

Problem

How do you design a replication to transmit data from the source to the target and from the target to the source when the common replication set is updateable on both sides during the replication interval?

Forces

Any of the following **compelling forces** would justify using the solution described in this pattern:

- **Need for updateable copies when not connected.** The application at the target has to be able to update data even if the source database is not reachable.
- **Optimistic concurrency control.** You have chosen to allow updates to a replication set without attempting distributed data updates to the corresponding replication set to keep it consistent (for example, because the computers are not permanently connected to each other). This is called optimistic concurrency control because it assumes that conflicts will arise but that these conflicts will be kept to a minimum. For this reason, conflict detection and resolution is necessary.

  If you cannot afford the risk of conflicts, you may choose to use the *Pessimistic Concurrency Control* pattern. (Both *Optimistic Concurrency Control* and *Pessimistic Concurrency Control* are patterns described in *Patterns of Enterprise Application Architecture* [Fowler03].)

The following **enabling forces** facilitate the adoption of the solution, and their absence may hinder such a move:

- **Tolerance of latency.** The applications on both source and target can cope with the fact that changes by other applications may not be visible immediately.
- **Network efficiency.** Network characteristics, such as reliability, bandwidth, and network latency (responsiveness), allow the participating databases to exchange replication data with sufficient speed. The expected rate of transmissions will not saturate the network connection.

- **Low likelihood of conflicts.** If the copies of the same item are updated on both source and target within the same transmission interval, the conflict has to be resolved, which results in one update overruling the other. Performing this conflict resolution consumes processing resources. If this additional workload is likely to be a problem for the target, then to use this pattern the likelihood of such conflicts should be fairly low.

Solution

Copy data from the source to the target and detect and resolve any update conflicts that have occurred since the last replication (due to changes to the same data on the source and target).

The solution consists of a replication building block with two replication links between the source and the target in opposite directions. Both replication links transmit the same replication set in both directions (see Figure 3.15). Such a pair of replication links is referred to as related links in the more detailed patterns.

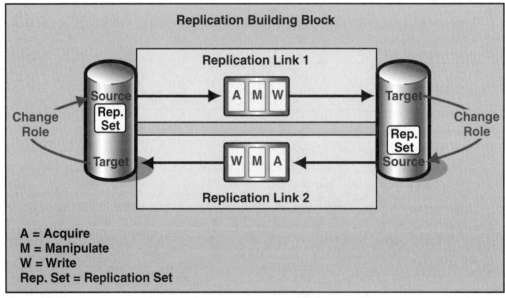

Figure 3.15
Master-Master Replication with related links

Before describing the elements of the replication building block in detail, some definitions and background are presented.

Replication Unit

A *replication unit* is the smallest amount of data that can be discretely recognized in the transmission set. The replication unit can be one of the following:

- Complete replication set
- Table of the replication set
- Transaction
- Row
- Column

For *Master-Master Replication*, the replication unit is almost always an individual row. In rare cases, it can also be a single column in a row, or it can be a complete transaction that has been executed on the source as well. The replication unit should not be the complete replication set or complete tables for a master-master replication.

Conflicts

During a transmission, special care has to be taken before the acquired and manipulated data is written to the target. Because the target can also be written to by applications, the data on the target may have been changed since the last transmission. A conflict occurs when data of a replication unit is also updated on the target since the last transmission. Before actually writing the replication unit to the target, conflicts must be detected and resolved.

Conflicts belong to one of the following categories:

- *Update conflicts* occur when the target data to be updated or deleted was updated after the last transmission.
- *Delete conflicts* occur when the target data to be updated or deleted was deleted after the last transmission.
- *Uniqueness conflicts* occur when the target data to be inserted or updated causes a violation of a uniqueness constraint, such as a duplicate key or a violation of a unique secondary index.
- *Business conflicts* occur when the data can be transmitted to the target, but the overall integrity of the target database would be violated by the written data.

The following is an example of a business conflict:

The database contains information about citizens, such as name, address, age, and driver's licenses. The business constraint states that all holders of driver's licenses must be at least 18 years old. Originally, both databases contain a record for John Smith, 20 years old, with no driver's license. Before the next transmission, both databases are updated by applications. In the source database, John is assigned a driver's license, which is acceptable because he is over 18 years old. In the target database his age is changed to 15 years, which is acceptable because he has no driver's license. Hence, both individual transactions meet the business constraint. After exchanging the updates, both databases would hold an entry for John Smith, 15 years old, with a driver's license. This violates the business constraint.

Conflict Detection

Before the transmitted data is actually written to the target, the corresponding data in the target has to be checked for potential conflicts. This conflict detection is always done on a row or column level, even if the replication unit is a complete transaction.

After a conflict has been detected, it must be resolved before writing the transmitted data.

Conflict Resolution

Methods for resolving conflicts may be simple or complex, depending on the business needs. Table 3.2 lists possible conflict resolution methods.

Table 3.2: Conflict Resolution Methods

Conflict	Method	Description
Update, delete	Priority based	Every database has a priority assigned to it. The replication unit from the database with the higher priority prevails.
Update	Value based	Rules defined on the values decide the winning replication unit. For example, if the data contains a timestamp, the more recent timestamp prevails.
Update	Merge	The values of both source and target are merged by operations such as: min, max sum, average
Update, delete	Overwrite	The data in the target database is overwritten in every case. Unlike the priority-based method, this method does not require conflict detection.
All	Manual	After a conflict is detected, the replication is suspended until the conflict is resolved manually.
Uniqueness	Discard	If you try to insert data that exists in the target database, the new data is ignored.
Uniqueness	Append sequence	If you try to insert data that exists in the target database, the key value is changed to a new value. Such data must be merged manually later.

In general, business conflicts cannot be resolved automatically. Instead, there are two ways to handle such conflicts:

- The data violating the business constraints are accepted temporarily in the target database. Usually, such data is marked during the transmission and must be cleansed manually.

- If temporary violations of business constraints are not acceptable, the replication must be suspended until the conflict is resolved manually.

Elements of Master-Master Replication

This section presents the elements of a *Master-Master Replication* solution in more detail.

Source and Target

Both source and target are databases containing a replication set. In general, the schemas of the source replication set and the target replication set may differ slightly, as long as the manipulate service can convert the data as described in the architectural replication pattern. However, for *Master-Master Replication*, the schemas are usually identical.

Hint: You should avoid using referential integrity in a *Master-Master Replication* scenario because it can give you major problems. You must ensure that the replication data is written to the databases without side effects, such as double updates due to referential integrity. This is very complex when you have referential integrity on both masters because of the two-way data exchange for the same set of data.

To ensure integrity, the source and target databases must not fire any follow-up operations, such as triggers or cascade deletes, during the replication (if the transmission from the source includes those changes as part of its change information). However, if you **must** have referential integrity constraints or triggers for other updates, then you have to prevent the transmission from triggering these operations. You can achieve this by using a dedicated user or role for the transmission and implementing the triggered operations so that they do not perform follow-up operations for the given user or role.

Acquire

Master-Master Replication does not overwrite the data in the target but tolerates changes in both databases. Thus, the transmission will send only the data changes, instead of the complete content of the replication set. That is, it performs an incremental replication, either as described in the *Master-Slave Transactional Incremental Replication* pattern, or an incremental replication on a row level. However, *Master-Slave Snapshot Replication* is not suitable for a master-master replication. Hence, the Acquire service will read only the changes to the replication set at the source.

Manipulate

The *Manipulate* service receives the data from Acquire. It can manipulate the data by performing operations on the fields of the current row and assign the result to an output field.

Typical uses of these expressions are:

- Data type conversions
- Concatenation of fields, for example first name and last name, into a single name field
- Splitting fields, for example extracting first name and last name from a name field

Because there is another replication link in the opposite direction, all manipulations of the data must be reversible; for example, the opposite replication link must perform complimentary manipulations of this service.

Write

The *Write* service receives the data to be written from the Manipulate service. Before actually writing a replication unit, it must check whether the corresponding target data has also changed since the last transmission. Therefore Write reads the appropriate data and performs the conflict detection. If a conflict has been detected, an appropriate conflict resolution method must be called, which either returns the winner or a new replication unit is written instead of the original one. If the changes from the source are accepted by the conflict resolution, or if a modified replication unit has been returned, this replication unit is to be written to the target. However, if the conflict resolution rejects the replication unit from the source, it must be discarded and not written to the target.

Example: Synchronizing Laptops and a Central Database

For example, you have a central database with customer data. Sales forces have all or parts of the database contents on their laptops to permit access to the data while disconnected from the network.

Both the central database and laptop databases can update customer data, such as addresses. When the sales force is back in the office, they synchronize the changes in their databases with any changes made to the central database since they were last connected.

Master-Master Replication allows the exchange of changes in both directions. An appropriate conflict resolution must be defined, for example the most recent change should overrule any older changes.

A similar scenario is described in more detail in the pattern *Master-Master Row-Level Synchronization*.

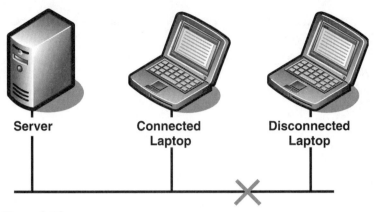

Figure 3.16
Central database and laptop databases

Resulting Context

As described in the previous section, the main problem in a master-master replication is the handling of conflicts. The complexity of the conflict resolution depends, among other things, on the replication unit.

If the replication units are complete transactions, it may be hard to resolve the conflicts automatically because non-trivial transactions might affect different tables in a manner such that no definite winner can be determined. In most cases, you will be forced to use the overwrite method or a manual resolution.

Hint: Use a replication unit of rows, if possible. Use columns only when absolutely necessary.

The replication refresh policy for a master-master replication will be an incremental replication because you have to be able to identify the changes at both source and target.

This pattern inherits the benefits and liabilities from *Data Replication* and has the following additional benefit and liabilities:

Benefits

- **Backup.** *Master-Master Replication* can be used as a means of backup. If one of the databases crashes, only changes made to this specific database since the last transmission will be lost.

Liabilities

- **Consistent conflict resolution methods.** The conflict resolution methods of both replication links must agree on the same result. For example, if you are using a priority-based conflict resolution where the priority for the source is 1 and for the target is 2, the value of the source will prevail. This same priority schema must be applied to each replication link.

- **Surveillance of conflict resolution.** The conflict resolution method should log its actions. This log must be checked regularly to ensure that the conflict resolution works correctly and the frequency of conflicts does not increase dramatically.

Next Considerations

During a more detailed design, the parameters of the replication have to be specified, for example:

- **Transmission frequency.** What is the appropriate timing of the transmission for the requirements?
- **Initiator.** Should the source push the transmission or should the target pull the transmission?

Related Patterns

For more information, see the following related patterns:

Patterns That May Have Led You Here

- *Move Copy of Data.* This pattern is the root pattern of this cluster; it presents the overall architecture to maintain redundant data by asynchronous writing of copies of data eventually after the data has been updated.
- *Data Replication.* This pattern presents the architecture of a replication.

Patterns That You Can Use Next

- *Master-Master Row-Level Synchronization.* This pattern presents a design for *Master-Master Replication*, which detects and resolves any conflicts at the row level.

Other Patterns of Interest

- *Master-Slave Replication.* This pattern presents an alternative to *Master-Master Replication*, where applications must not write to the target; otherwise, such updates will be overwritten by a later transmission.
- *Master-Slave Snapshot Replication.* This pattern presents a design for transmitting a complete replication set. This can be used to equalize both databases as a starting point before establishing a master-master replication.

Acknowledgments

[Fowler03] Fowler, Martin. *Patterns of Enterprise Application Architecture.* Addison-Wesley, 2003

Master-Slave Replication

Context

You are about to design a replication building block with a source and a target that meet the following requirements:

- Replication set at the source is being updated by applications.
- Replication set at the target is either read-only or updateable; however, any changes made to the target replication set will not be transmitted back to the source and may be overwritten by a subsequent replication.

Problem

How do you design the replication building block to transmit data from the source to the target and apply appropriate overwrite rules on the target?

Forces

Any of the following **compelling forces** would justify using the solution described in this pattern:

- **Simplicity.** You have no reason to use a more complex solution, and you avoid any potential referential integrity problems.

The following **enabling forces** facilitate the move to the solution, and their absence may hinder such a move:

- **Tolerance of overwrites.** If some data has been updated by an application on the target, it might eventually be replaced by data from the source.
- **Stability.** The target applications require data that is stable over a predictable period, and may only change at defined points in time.

Solution

Copy data from the source to the target without regard to updates that may have occurred to the replication set at the target since the last replication.

Master-Slave Replication uses a single replication building block, as shown in Figure 3.17 on the next page.

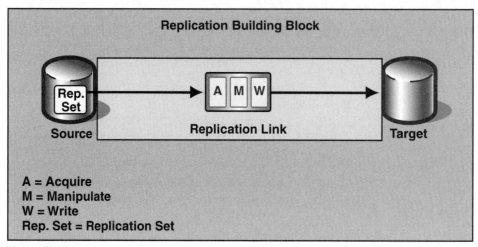

Figure 3.17
Master-Slave Replication

The replication link reads the data or its changes from the source, manipulates them for the target structure, and then writes them to the target.

Source

The source database contains the replication set to be copied.

Acquire

The *Acquire* service reads the contents of the replication set from the source to get the data to be transmitted. The source is either the data itself or a log of its changes. A replication that transmits only the changes is called an incremental replication. A replication that transmits the entire replication set on every transmission is called a snapshot replication. For a detailed description, see the corresponding patterns.

Hint: Acquiring only the changes is preferred when the following conditions are true:

● The average number of changes during a transmission interval is relatively small compared to the size of the replication set.

● Appropriate means to detect or record the changes on the source are present or can be implemented.

If these conditions are not true, transmission of the entire replication set is preferred.

Manipulate

The *Manipulate* service receives the data or its changes from Acquire. It can manipulate the data by performing operations on the fields of the current row, and then assigning the result to an output field.

Typical uses of such operations are:

- Data type conversions
- Concatenation of fields, for example first name and last name, into a single name field
- Splitting fields, for example extracting first name and last name from a name field

Write

The resulting rows of Manipulate are used by the Write services to update the target database in one of the following manners:

- In a one-way replication with overwrite, any existing data on the target can be replaced by the new data.
- In a one-way replication with no overwrite, the existing data on the target are compared to the new data. If they differ, the new data is appended as a new version. If they are identical, no write is needed.

Hint: *Master-Slave Cascading Replication* is the typical deployment of *Master-Slave Replication*.

Target

The target is the database, where the transmitted and possibly manipulated data or changes are written.

Hint: You must ensure that the data is written to the target without side effects, such as double updates due to referential integrity. Hence, the target database must not fire any follow-up operations, such as triggers or cascade deletes, during the replication (if the transmission from the source includes those changes as part of its change information). However, if you need referential integrity or triggers for application updates that affect the replication set, you must prevent the replication from triggering these operations. You can achieve this, for example, by using a dedicated user or role for the transmission and by implementing the triggered operations so that they do not perform follow-up operations for the given user or role.

Examples

The following paragraphs show two examples of *Master-Slave Replication*. The first example deals with slow network connections and the second one shows how to divide operational and reporting databases.

Remote Read-Only Access Across a Low Bandwidth Connection

Some of your applications need read-only access to the data, but the network connection does not have enough bandwidth capacity to meet the required response times for user queries.

The solution is to replicate the database to a server in a network segment that can provide a higher bandwidth service for these applications. Because the applications only read the data, a master-slave replication will keep the target up-to-date. The replication should be designed as an incremental replication that transmits the changes from the source to the target as soon as possible.

The *Master-Slave Transactional Incremental Replication* pattern presents the design of such a particular master-slave replication.

Operational Database and Reporting Database

You have an operational database with ongoing updates by applications, and you need a stable view on last day's state of the database for reporting purposes. You decided to have two separated databases, one for the ongoing operations and one for reporting.

Master-Slave Replication allows you to transmit the data from the operational database to the reporting database every night. On the following day, the reporting database reflects the state of the operational database of the previous day. It will not change until the next transmission.

The transmission from the source to the target can be done with snapshots if the time period reserved for the transmission is sufficient to extract the snapshot from the source and to transfer it and write it to the target. The design of *Snapshot Replication* is presented in its own pattern.

Resulting Context

Because of the nature of a master-slave replication, changes to the target that have been made by applications exist until they are overwritten by a later transmission. If the replication only transmits the changes from the source, local changes on the target might remain even after a transmission. This occurs if the corresponding data has not been changed on the source, and thus the data is not transmitted and does not replace any data on the target.

After you decide to apply the *Master-Slave Replication* pattern, the following considerations will lead you to a more detailed design:

- **Transmission frequency.** Define the appropriate timing of the transmission to meet the requirements.

- **Transmission volume.** Define the right amount of data to transmit. For example, you could send all individual changes for a particular record, or just the aggregated result of them over the period, or the entire replication set.

- **Replication Unit.** Define the smallest updating operation that will be transmitted from the source to the target. In very strong requirements, this will be a transaction as it has been executed on the source. A weaker but easier to achieve requirement is to move a changed record. For environments with a high risk of conflicts, it might also be an individual change of a column within a record.

- **Initiator.** Decide whether the source will push the transmission or the target will pull it.

The use of this pattern inherits the benefits and liabilities from *Data Replication* and has the following additional benefits and liabilities:

Benefits

- **Simplicity.** *Master-Slave Replication* is substantially easier to design and implement than Master-Master Replication, which allows applications to update the target, but which has to cope with conflicts.

- **Stable view on the database contents.** For a stable view on the data, you can transmit the data to dedicated target database, which will not experience any updates, as long as you need the data to be frozen. This allows you to investigate the stable data in the target database, while ongoing operations change the contents of the source database. Without a master-slave replication, you would have to enrich the schema to access historical data.

- **Backup.** *Master-Slave Replication* with an automatic transmission to the target can be used as a means of backup. If the source needs to be recovered, the content of the target can be moved back to the source. Only the changes since the last transmission will be lost.

Liabilities

- **Growing storage needs with one-way replication with no target overwrite.** Because this variant creates new versions whenever the transmitted data differs from the existing data on the target, space requirements constantly grow. You must monitor the storage consumption and eventually delete old versions, possibly after archiving them.

Related Patterns

For more information, see the following related patterns:

Patterns That May Have Led You Here

- *Move Copy of Data.* This is the root pattern of this cluster; it presents the overall architecture to maintain redundant data by asynchronous writing of copies of data after the data has been updated.
- *Data Replication.* This pattern presents the architecture of a replication.

Patterns That You Can Use Next

- *Master-Slave Snapshot Replication.* This pattern presents a solution that transmits the whole replication set from the source to the target on each transmission.
- *Master-Slave Transactional Incremental Replication.* This pattern presents a solution that transmits only the changes from the source to the target on a transaction-by-transaction basis.

Other Patterns of Interest

- *Master-Master Replication.* This pattern presents an alternative to *Master-Slave Replication*, where the target may be written by applications, and such updates are transmitted back to the source.
- *Master-Slave Cascading Replication.* This pattern shows how *Master-Slave Replication* can be applied iteratively in more complex topologies.

Master-Master Row-Level Synchronization

Context

You are about to design a replication between a source and a target, as described in *Master-Master Replication*. Your requirements are:

- The replication set is updateable at either end of the replication.
- Updates need to be transmitted to the other party.
- Conflicts need to be detected and resolved at defined points in time, following defined data integrity rules.
- Potential conflicts in the changes are to be resolved at the row level.

Note: This pattern uses relational database terms to discuss the solution, but the solution will work in other contexts. The pattern also assumes the existence of relational database management system (RDBMS) services, such as change logging.

Problem

How do you design a replication to transmit data from the source to the target and vice versa, when the same replication set is updateable at either end of the replication and you want to resolve conflicts at the row level?

Forces

All of the forces that were described in the *Master-Master Replication* pattern apply in this context, and there is one additional one. The relevant forces are repeated here for convenience.

Any of the following **compelling forces** would justify using the solution described in this pattern:

- **Need for updateable copies when not connected.** The application at the target has to be able to update data even if the source database is not reachable.
- **Optimistic concurrency control.** You have chosen to allow updates to a replication set without attempting distributed data updates to the corresponding replication set to keep it consistent (for example, because the computers are not permanently connected to each other). This is called optimistic concurrency control because it assumes that conflicts will occur but that they will be few in number. This type of concurrency control requires that you use conflict detection and resolution methods.

  If you cannot afford the risk of conflicts, you may choose to use the Pessimistic Concurrency Control pattern. (Both Optimistic Concurrency Control and Pessimistic Concurrency Control are patterns described in [Fowler03].)

The following **enabling forces** facilitate the adoption of the solution, and their absence may hinder such a move:

- **Tolerance of latency.** The applications on both source and target can cope with the fact that changes by other applications may not be visible immediately.

- **Network efficiency.** Network characteristics, such as reliability, bandwidth, and network latency (responsiveness) allow the participating databases to exchange replication data with sufficient speed. The expected rate of transmissions will not saturate the network connection.

- **Low likelihood of conflicts.** If the copies of the same item are updated on both source and target within the same transmission interval, the conflict has to be resolved, which results in one update overruling the other. Performing this conflict resolution consumes processing resources. If this additional workload is likely to be a problem for the target, then to use this pattern the likelihood of such conflicts should be fairly low.

- **Well-defined synchronization times.** There are well-defined points in time where the relevant parts of the databases can be brought into consistency. For example, whenever a laptop is connected to the corporate network, the replication process is started automatically or manually.

Solution

Create a pair of related replication links between the source and target as described in the *Master-Master Replication* pattern. Additionally, create a synchronization controller to manage the synchronization and connect the links. This solution describes the function of one of these replication links. The other replication link behaves the same way, but in the opposite direction. To synchronize more than two copies of the replication set, create the appropriate replication link pair for each additional copy.

Hint: When designing the replication link, it is important to know what types of conflicts can occur and how to handle them so that the integrity of replicated data remains intact. The design of conflict detection and conflict resolution is described in the *Master-Master Replication* pattern.

Figure 3.18 shows the use of the replication building block and its elements to design the solution for master-master synchronization, and the added services to manage the relationship between the pair of links.

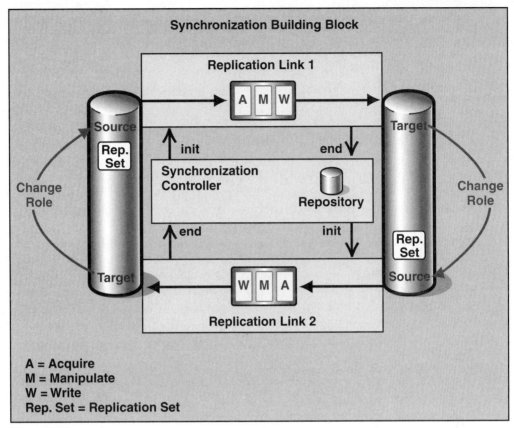

Figure 3.18
Master-Master Synchronization using two related replication links

Controller

The synchronization building block is an extension of the replication building block and consists of two replication links and a synchronization controller. The controller manages the synchronization and relates the replication link pair.

The controller uses a small repository to keep track of the transactions. This repository contains information about the replication links and the transmissions on each of them. Figure 3.19 on the next page shows a data model for this repository.

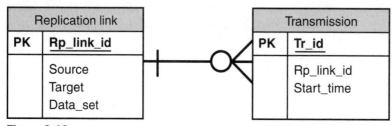

Figure 3.19
Database design for handling synchronization data

At the start of every transmission, the controller reads the start time of the last synchronization for this replication link from the repository. It then invokes the Acquire service to get the replication set from the source. The controller waits until the Write service notifies it that it has written the replication set to the target, and then the controller invokes the Acquire service of the second replication link to get the target's replication set. This replication set now serves as the source for the second link, and the source for the first link now serves as the target for the second link. When the transmission is complete, the Write service of the second link notifies the controller. Finally, the controller writes the start time for this synchronization into the repository, which shows that the synchronization is complete.

Source/Target

To use this pattern, you must ensure that the following is true on the source and target:

- Every table in the replication set has a replication key. A replication key is either the unique key that identifies the table or a combination of columns that uniquely identifies each row.

- Any rows that have been updated are marked as such. To mark a row, you typically use a timestamp, which indicates the date and time of the change. If the change is a DELETE, you do not actually delete the source row yet. Instead, you add a delete flag either on the row itself, or in an additional table (see the Hint following this list) with the same keys. If you store the keys of deleted rows in an additional table, you can delete the rows from the main table and synchronize on the shadow tables. You must ensure that applications never read rows with the delete flag set.

- Clocks of the participating computers are nearly synchronized. To avoid problems caused by different time zones, all timestamps should use the same time zone.

- The application does not change the unique key that the synchronization uses; instead, the application deletes the row with the old value and inserts a row with new values.

Hint: Marking updates requires that you add columns to the existing tables. If you cannot add these columns, then you need to create a shadow table for every table in the replication set. These have the same primary keys as the main tables and they store the date/timestamps, and delete flags. Changes to these tables need to be synchronized too.

When the application makes changes to the rows of the source, it also writes information for the replication link to use, as Table 3.3 shows.

Table 3.3: Additional Application Actions to Identify the Replication Set

Operation	Action
INSERT	The new row is marked for transmission by the next transmission.
UPDATE	The updated row is marked for transmission by the next transmission.
DELETE	The deleted row is marked and logged, and is kept for the next transmission.

If you are using an RDBMS, you can use one of the following means to mark and log the rows without changing the application:

- The logging system of the underlying RDBMS (in this case, no changes to database schemas are required)
- Additional artifacts in the database, such as triggers (this requires database schema changes)

Acquire

In this pattern, the Acquire service is invoked by the controller module and is passed its context. It reads the replication set to get the rows that have been changed or marked as deleted since the last transmission.

Manipulate

There are no special considerations for the Manipulate service in a synchronization environment other than all manipulations of the data must be reversible. This is because the related replication link must perform the complementary manipulations of this service. For example, if you concatenate a bank code number and an account number in the first transmission, then you must be able to split this string on the reverse transmission.

Write

Since the solution uses optimistic concurrency control, the Write service must check for conflicts before writing to the target. Methods for conflict detection and resolution are presented in the *Master-Master Replication* pattern.

If a conflict has been detected, an appropriate conflict resolution method must be called, which either returns the winner or a new row to be written instead of the original one. If the conflict resolution method accepts changes from the source, or if it returns a modified row, this row is to be written to the target. However, if the conflict resolution rejects the row from the source, it must be discarded and must not be written to the target.

Hint: Use of DELETE flags leads to a need for cleanup, which means that at some point you need to physically delete these rows from all the copies that they exist in. To do this, each copy needs to know the synchronization times for all directly related replications so that it can use these times to know which rows can safely be deleted. Rows whose timestamp is older than any of the related synchronization times can be deleted.

Example

This example outlines a common implementation of the *Master-Master Row-Level Synchronization* pattern. The replication unit is a row. The rows in the replication set are marked with a timestamp and a delete flag. Hence, every table has two additional columns. The applications must not read any rows that are marked as deleted, and it should never read the additional columns (that is, do not use statements such as SELECT * FROM).

Figure 3.20 shows the algorithm for detecting and resolving conflicts when timestamps and delete flags are used. In this case, the most recent timestamp wins. If the row in the transmission has the most recent timestamp, it is written to the target. If it doesn't, the target row is left untouched and the transmission row is discarded. Overall integrity will be restored when the related replication link runs.

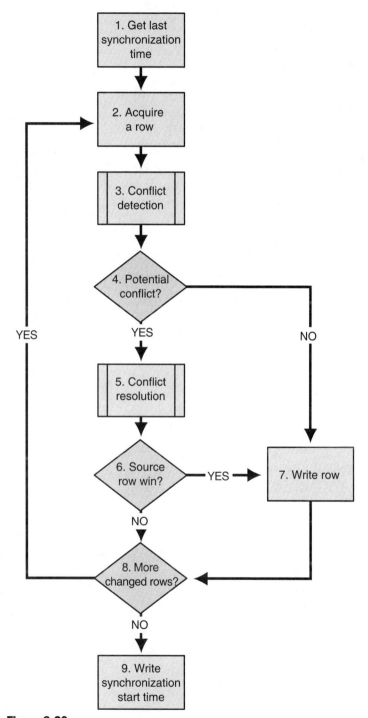

Figure 3.20
Synchronization algorithm for most recent timestamp wins

The following list provides more information about each step in the algorithm shown in Figure 3.20.

▶ **Algorithm using timestamps for conflict detection**

1. Get the last synchronization time from the Controller.

2. Acquire a row from the replication set.

3. Conflict detection: Check the corresponding target row to see if it has been changed since the last synchronization by comparing the target timestamp with the synchronization timestamp.

4. Potential conflict?

   No: If the timestamp of the target row is older than the synchronization timestamp, the row has not changed and you can write the UPDATE; skip to step 7.

   If there is no corresponding target row, then assume this is an INSERT and skip to step 7.

   Yes: If the target row has changed, use conflict resolution.

5. Conflict resolution: Apply the conflict resolution rules. This example uses the "latest timestamp" rule, so compare the target row timestamp and the transmission row timestamp.

6. Source row win?

   Yes: If the timestamp on the transmission row from the source is more recent, proceed to step 7.

   No: Discard the transmission row and skip to step 8.

7. Write the transmission row to the target.

8. More changed rows?

   Yes: If there are more changed rows, repeat the sequence beginning at step 2.

   No: If there are no more changed rows, proceed to step 9.

9. Write the start time of the synchronization into the Controller metadata.

An implementation of a synchronization with row-level conflict resolution based on the services of Microsoft® SQL Server™ is presented in *Implementing Master-Master Row-Level Synchronization Using SQL Server*.

Resulting Context

This pattern inherits the benefits and liabilities of the *Data Replication* and the *Master-Master Replication* patterns, which are not repeated here. It also has one additional liability.

Additional Liability

Cleanup after synchronization of DELETE operations. During synchronization you must not physically delete the rows until the information about the deletion is transmitted to targets. Eventually, after all transmissions are complete, you should physically delete the rows.

Operational Considerations

When using *Master-Master Row-Level Synchronization,* you must ensure that the transmissions do not interfere with normal operations. This can be achieved by one of these alternatives:

- Lock the participating databases to prevent any other update activity.
- Perform the whole synchronization within a database transaction, and thereby isolate it from any other activity.
- Store the timestamp of when the synchronization started. This ensures that changes made by transactions that run concurrently with the synchronization are not missed. Changes made by those transactions are sent by the next synchronization.

Related Patterns

For more information, see the following related patterns:

Patterns That May Have Led You Here

- *Move Copy of Data.* This pattern is the root pattern of this cluster; it presents the overall architecture for maintaining copies of data.
- *Data Replication.* This pattern presents the architecture of data replication, which is a particular way of moving copies of data.
- *Master-Master Replication.* This pattern presents the high-level solution for a data replication where there is bidirectional data movement between source and target. This includes conflict detection and resolution to handle concurrent updates to different copies of the same data in the same transmission interval.

Patterns That You Can Use Next

- *Implementing Row-Level Synchronization Using SQL Server* presents the pattern for implementing a row-level synchronization by using SQL Server.

Other Patterns of Interest

- *Master-Slave Snapshot Replication.* This pattern presents a design for transmitting a full replication set (not just changes). This can be used to equalize the source and target sets as a starting point before establishing a synchronization relationship.

Acknowledgments

[Fowler03] Fowler, Martin. *Patterns of Enterprise Application Architecture.* Addison-Wesley, 2003

Master-Slave Snapshot Replication

Context

You have to design a replication solution for these requirements:

- A replication set is to be copied from a single source to a target, and possibly to more than one target. The replication set consists of entire rows, not just changes that have occurred to rows since the last replication.

- Any changes made to the replication data at the target that may have occurred since the last transmission will be overwritten by a new transmission. Hence, the snapshot replication is a master-slave replication.

Problem

How do you move an entire replication set from source to target so that it is consistent at a given point in time?

Forces

All of the forces described in the *Master-Slave Replication* pattern and its parent patterns apply in this context, and there are additional forces that apply. The relevant *Master-Slave Replication* forces are repeated here for convenience.

Any of the following **compelling forces** justify using the solution described in this pattern:

- **Simplicity.** You have no reason to use a more complex solution, and you avoid any potential referential integrity problems.

- **High ratio of changes.** The ratio of replication set changes to overall volume of the replication set content is substantial. On every transmission, most of the replication set has changed. Therefore, it makes more sense to transmit the whole replication set, rather than just parts of it. In this case, operational resources are saved by performing a snapshot replication.

The following **enabling forces** facilitate the move to the solution, and their absence may hinder such a move:

- **Tolerance of overwrites.** If some data has been updated by an application on the target, it might eventually be replaced by data from the source.

- **Stability.** The target applications require data that is stable over a predictable period, and may only change at defined points in time.

- **Initial database load.** You need to perform an initial population of a target database; therefore, the whole source replication set must be transmitted. For this reason, it makes sense to use a snapshot replication before using other types of replication.

Solution

Make a copy of the source replication set at a specific time (this is known as a *snapshot*), replicate it to the target, and overwrite the target data. In this way, any changes that may have occurred to the target replication set are replaced by the new source replication set.

Master-Slave Snapshot Replication uses a single replication building block, consisting of the source, the replication link with Acquire, Manipulate, and Write, and Figure 3.21 shows the target.

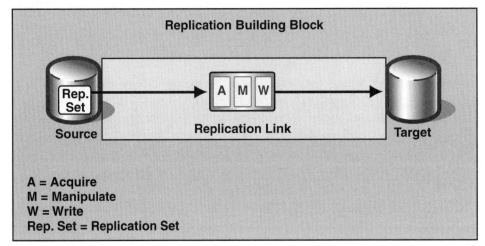

Figure 3.21
Snapshot replication

Source

The source database contains the replication set to be transmitted.

Acquire

In the *Master-Slave Snapshot Replication* pattern, the replications set that is acquired consists of the full set of complete rows that are to be copied to the target (not just the changes that were made to the data at the source).

Manipulate

The dimension of possible data manipulations in a *Master-Slave Snapshot Replication* environment depends on the implementation.

Hint: The snapshot replication between databases can be performed either by a direct connection with SQL statements or by the use of an extract tool. If the snapshot replication uses a tool, a separate manipulation service needs data in an accessible structure to read and change the replication set. Thus, manipulations can be done if the format of the extracted file is documented (for example, extracts to text files). Binary files cannot be used by this service.

Write

The replication set is written to the target by the Write service without checking for updates to the target. To write the replication set, the service can use one of the following options, depending upon the circumstances at the target:

- The relevant target tables are dropped and new ones are created before inserting the replication set.

- All data in the existing tables is overwritten. The tables are truncated before the replication set is written.

- The service deletes the old replication set on the target and writes the new replication set.

The first and the second option can be used if the target mirrors the source. The last option is appropriate if data exists in addition to the replication set, and this data must not be affected by the replication.

Hint: The *Master-Slave Snapshot Replication* does not depend on a network connection between the source and the target. If no such connection exists, or its characteristics, such as bandwidth, are not sufficient, the acquired snapshot can be written to removable media. Removable media, such as compact discs, are then transported to the target, where the snapshot is written to the target.

Target

The target is the database where the transmitted replication set to be written.

Example

A common use of *Master-Slave Snapshot Replication* is to establish a starting point for other replications, for example, incremental replication or synchronization. In this case, an identical state of the content of the replication set is needed on the source and the target to ensure data consistency when transmitting changes.

Resulting Context

The pattern inherits the benefits and liabilities from the *Master-Slave Replication* and it has the following additional benefits and liabilities:

Benefits

- **Provides data at a well-defined point in time.** All data of the replicated replication set is assigned to an exact point in time. This information can be used for historical or analytical issues. In these cases, a snapshot replication provides you with a consistent, nonvolatile data basis.

- **Low resource consumption during operational work.** *Master-Slave Snapshot Replication* does not check for updates to the data. Hence, during the Write, this type of replication requires fewer resources than incremental replication.

- **Independence of network connections.** If you have to replicate a large data volume, and the infrastructure provides only a low-speed communication link, snapshot replication using removable media allows you to bypass these restrictions.

Liabilities

- **High resource consumption during transmission.** Because the whole replication set is transmitted even if only small parts of the source replication set changed during the replication interval, a higher network load occurs and more working disk space is needed. The pressure of this problem grows with the volume of replicated data.

- **Need a time frame to apply the snapshot.** Especially if you replicate a large volume of data, it takes a certain time to acquire the snapshot from the source. To keep the replication set on the source consistent, it must not be changed by running applications during this time period. You can achieve this either by avoiding write operations from the application or by locking the data so that the replication set cannot be updated during the snapshot transmission. Otherwise, the data consistency cannot be guaranteed.

Security Considerations

Snapshot data can reside in places other than the source and target data. Snapshot data requires security standards that are as high as the security standards used for the source and the target.

Related Patterns

For more information, see the following related patterns:

Patterns That May Have Led You Here

- *Move Copy of Data.* This pattern is the root pattern of this cluster. It presents the fundamental data movement building block, which consists of source, data movement set, data movement link, and target. Transmissions in this kind of data movement building block are done asynchronously, sometime after the update of the source. Thus, the target applications must tolerate a certain amount of latency until changes are delivered.
- *Data Replication.* This pattern presents the architecture of a replication, which is a specific type of data copy movement.
- *Master-Slave Replication.* This pattern describes design considerations for transmitting data from the source to the target by overwriting potential changes in the target on a higher level than the *Master-Slave Snapshot Replication.*

Patterns That You Can Use Next

- *Implementing Master-Slave Snapshot Replication Using SQL Server.* This pattern shows how to implement *Master-Slave Snapshot Replication* by using Microsoft® SQL Server™.

Patterns of Interest

- *Master-Master Replication.* This pattern presents the design of a replication between a source and a target, where the common replication set is updateable at either end.
- *Master-Slave Transactional Incremental Replication.* This pattern also describes a master-slave replication at a design level. It differs from the *Master-Slave Snapshot Replication* in that it transmits only changes of data from the source to the target using transactions.

Capture Transaction Details

Context

You are about to design a replication link using *Master-Slave Transactional Incremental Replication*. For this purpose, you need access to transactional information on the source, and a logging system will not fulfill this need for one of the following reasons:

- There is a logging system available at the source database but for some good reasons you do not want to use it.
- You do not have access to a logging system.

In these cases, you need to design the recording of transactions on the source with your own artifacts.

Note: This pattern presumes knowledge of the concepts, terms, and definitions of the *Data Replication* architectural pattern, from which this pattern inherits concepts and terms.

Problem

How do you design a recording of transactional information for all changes to a source replication set?

Forces

Any of the following **compelling forces** justify using the solution described in this pattern:

- **No access to transactional information.** You cannot access transactional information in the logging system because either you are not using a database system at the source, or the database system does not provide access to the transaction log.
- **Transactional information is not suitable.** The information provided might be usable in the originating database only, for example, because it contains physical addresses instead of key values and thus cannot be applied on the target.

The following **enabling force** facilitates the adoption of the solution, and its absence might hinder such a move:

- **Recording for other purposes.** Recording of transactions is required for other purposes, for example, auditing.

Solution

The solution is to create additional database objects, such as triggers and (shadow) tables, and to record changes of all tables belonging to the replication set.

The details of the solution are separated into:

- Prerequisites for recording transactional information
- Designing your own recording of transactions

Note: This pattern uses the terms "transactions" and "operations" with the following meanings:

A *transaction* is a collection of SQL commands that form a unit of work. Depending on the relational database management system (RDBMS), a transaction is started explicitly by a command like Begin Transaction, or implicitly by the first SQL command outside of a transaction. The transaction is ended either explicitly by a commit or a rollback, or implicitly at the end of every SQL command in autocommit mode.

An *operation* is the change (INSERT, UPDATE, or DELETE) of an individual row within a transaction.

Prerequisites

This pattern depends on two features that the database management system (DBMS) must provide, and on a prerequisite for the data model:

- **Fine-grained clock.** The order in which transactions are executed on the source must be the same as the order in which they are replayed on the target. Thus, the source clock must provide a sufficiently fine resolution to preserve the order. A clock grain of a millisecond is generally sufficient; many systems provide even microseconds. A clock that only has a resolution of whole seconds definitely prevents the use of this pattern.

- **Transaction Identifiers.** The RDBMS must provide a means to identify the operations that belong to the same transaction. This is called a *Transaction Identifier* throughout the remaining discussion. It is typically an opaque data type, and is generally provided to handle distributed transactions.

- **Unique key.** All tables of the replication set must have either unique keys or another combination of columns that identifies every row uniquely. The unique identifier of every row is referred to as the *Replication Key* throughout this document.

Designing Your Own Recording of Transactions

Since you cannot access the logging system of the source to acquire the transactional information, you have to implement the recording of the transactions using other DBMS services, such as triggers. Triggers are schema objects that perform additional operations on behalf of an initial operation. Triggered operations are also part of the initiating transaction and are logged in the same way as any other operation.

Hint: It is also possible to record transactions by changing the application to write a copy of the operation to a user-defined database, but this is very unusual.

The triggered function has to collect the following information for every committed transaction:

- Transaction Identifier
- Tables written to by the transaction
- For every table, the rows that have been written must be recorded. The data to be stored includes the current timestamp, the type of operation (INSERT, UPDATE, or DELETE) and additional information depending on the type of operation:
  - For INSERTs, the values of all fields must be recorded.
  - For UPDATEs that do not change the Replication Key, the new values of all changed columns, including the column names, must be recorded.
  - For UPDATEs that do change the Replication Key, the old and new values of the Replication Key must also be saved. Alternatively, you might record this as a DELETE of the old row followed by an INSERT of the new row, unless this approach violates integrity constraints.
  - For DELETEs, only the Replication Key of the deleted row is needed. If the DELETE fires cascade deletes of related rows, these additional deletes are recorded by further trigger invocations on those rows.
- Timestamp of when the transaction has been completed on the source. If you cannot fire a trigger on the COMMIT, you can use the timestamp of the last operation within the transaction instead.

To store the above information, you need a table for the transactions and three additional shadow tables for each table that belongs to the replication set. The shadow tables store the inserted, updated, and deleted rows. The three shadow tables can be combined into one by adding a column to store the type of operation; depending on the type of operation, some of the columns will be empty. Figure 3.22 shows the corresponding data model.

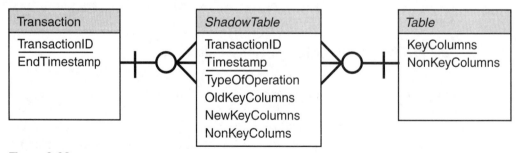

Figure 3.22
Data model to store transactional information

When an INSERT, UPDATE or DELETE is triggered, the following steps must be taken:

- Retrieve the Transaction Identifier of the current transaction.

- UPDATE the current date and time in the EndTimestamp for the current transaction in the Transaction table. If the UPDATE statement returns no updated row, the transaction is new. Thus, INSERT a new row with the Transaction Identifier and the current date and time.

- INSERT these values into the shadow table that corresponds to the table being written:

  - Transaction Identifier

  - Current date and time

  - Type of operation (INSERT, UPDATE, or DELETE)

  - Operation values:

    - For an INSERT: the value of all columns

    - For an UPDATE: the old and new key values plus the values of the remaining columns

    - For a DELETE: the old key values

Transactions that are rolled back do not affect the source, and consequently must not affect the target. For this reason, you do not want to store information about rolled back transactions. The recording of the transaction details should be done within the same transaction that is being recorded. Then if the transaction is rolled back, the recording of the transaction is rolled back as well. Thus, information about rolled-back transactions is not recorded.

Resulting Context

The use of this pattern has the following benefit and liability:

Benefit

- **Other useful services.** Recording transactions is very similar to other services, such as auditing. If the recorded information is enriched with data, such as current user or role, it can be the basis for auditing too.

Liability

- **Increasing space requirements.** Recording transactions writes new information into the transaction table and the shadow tables. Thus, the space requirements of these tables are constantly increasing. You should design and schedule a house-keeping process that removes the transactional information from these tables once they have been transmitted to the targets.

Next Considerations

The transactional information recorded by the use of this pattern can be used by *Master-Slave Transactional Incremental Replication*, which is a separate pattern.

Variants

If you feel that the resolution of your clock is fine enough to correctly order the transactions, but you do not trust the resolution to order the operations within the transaction, you can still use this pattern by following this variant. This variant also increases the efficiency of replaying the transactions on the target.

Combining Operations

The concept behind this variant is that the result of a transaction does not depend on the order of its operations, but rather upon the net effect on any particular row within the transaction. So if an application on the source writes the same record twice within a transaction, the operations on that row can be aggregated to a single operation to be applied to the target. If the source application writes more than twice to the same row in a transaction, each of the other rows again aggregate with the previous aggregation to create a new aggregated row.

The following table presents the aggregated operation that has to be stored to achieve the correct net effect of two operations on the same row identified by the replication key in a single transaction:

Table 3.4: Net Effects of Two Operations on the Same Row

		Second operation		
		INSERT	UPDATE	DELETE
First operation	INSERT	Impossible	Insert	Do nothing
	UPDATE	Impossible	Update	Delete
	DELETE	Update	Impossible	Impossible

The design of recording transactions on the source must now add these steps when storing the operation:

- Determine if there is an earlier operation on the same row within the same transaction.
- Determine the aggregated operation if an earlier operation is found.
- Store the recorded or combined operation.

When applying this variant you must not have any referential integrity constraints on the target because the operations of the transaction might be executed in a different order. This would violate such constraints temporarily.

When combining several operations on the same row into a single operation, updates of the Replication Key might become a problem. However, because the target does not have referential integrity constraints for the reason just given, an update of key values can be converted into a delete of the old row, followed by an insert of the new row.

Related Patterns

For more information, see the following related patterns:

Patterns That May Have Led You Here

- *Move Copy of Data.* This pattern is the root pattern of this cluster. It presents the fundamental data movement building block consisting of source, data movement set, data movement link, and target. Transmissions in such a data movement building block are done asynchronously some time after the update of the source. Thus, the target applications must tolerate a certain amount of latency until changes are delivered.

- *Data Replication.* This pattern presents the architecture of a replication, which is a specific type of data copy movement.

- *Master-Slave Replication.* This pattern presents the high-level design for a replication where changes at the source are transmitted to the target by overwriting potential updates of the target.

Patterns That You Can Use Next

- *Master-Slave Transactional Incremental Replication.* This pattern uses transactions to transmit changes from the source to the target. These changes might have been recorded using the *Capture Transaction Details* pattern.

Master-Slave Transactional Incremental Replication

Context

You are about to design the handling of transmissions on a replication link. Your requirements are:

- The replication set that you are sending to the target consists only of changes made to the source data, so you are designing an Incremental Replication.

- All needed data must be available to the target applications at any point in time; this includes related data such as reference data in other tables.

You have decided to achieve this by replicating the changes on a transactional level. Thus, you must retrieve transactional information from the source by either by accessing the transaction log of the database system or by preparing the source database as described in the *Capture Transactional Details* pattern. Since the granularity of a transmission is a transaction, both source and target have to be database management systems (DBMSs), which we will describe in relational DBMS (RDBMS) terms.

Note: This pattern uses concepts, terms, and definitions that are introduced in the *Data Replication* architectural pattern. It uses the services described in the *Capture Transaction Details* pattern as well.

Problem

How do you design a replication link to support the transmission of transactional changes, and to replay them on the target while meeting all integrity requirements?

Forces

Any of the following **compelling forces** justify using the solution described in this pattern:

- **Availability of consistent data on a complex target schema.** When applications read data from the target, all related data (for example, referenced data in other tables) must be available and consistently up-to-date. This requires that each transaction that updates the source be transmitted to the target as one transaction.

The following **enabling forces** facilitate the adoption of the solution, and their absence may hinder such a move:

- **Small volume of changes compared to the volume of the replication set.** The size of the changes being moved from the source to the target on each transmission is significantly smaller than the size of the replication set. Thus, the changes will be transmitted faster than a new snapshot of the replication set.

- **Similarity in the replication sets.** The schemas of both source and target must be nearly identical, although you can tolerate the following types of differences:
  - Different data types for corresponding columns at source and target.
  - One column of the source table can be split into different columns in the target table.
  - Several columns of the source table can be combined into a single column of the target table.

Solution

The solution is to acquire the information about committed transactions from the source and to replay the transactions in the correct sequence when they are written to the target.

Note: This pattern uses the terms 'transactions' and 'operations' with the following meanings:

A *transaction* is a collection of SQL commands that form a unit of work. Depending on the RDBMS, a transaction is started explicitly by a command like Begin Transaction, or implicitly by the first SQL command outside of a transaction. The transaction is ended either explicitly by a commit or a rollback, or implicitly at the end of every SQL command in autocommit mode.

An *operation* is the change (INSERT, UPDATE, or DELETE) of an individual row within a transaction.

Figure 3.23 shows the replication building block for this type of replication.

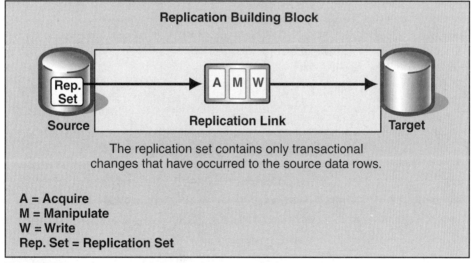

Figure 3.23
Replication building block for Master-Slave Transactional Incremental Replication

Depending on the features of the RDBMS and on the requirements of the replication link, the transactional information can be acquired either from the logging system of the source or from additional schema objects on the source. In both cases, the effects of the transaction are acquired as a collection of operations on the rows being updated by the transaction. The transmission to the target results in the corresponding rows being updated by transactions of the same size and in the correct sequence (according to their completion time at the source).

The detailed description of this pattern is separated into:

- Background
- Prerequisites for this pattern
- Recorded transactions executed on the target

Background

Before starting to describe the design of a transactional replication link, here are two considerations of more general nature:

- Transaction order for replay
- Handling triggers, if the Write service uses standard SQL

Transaction Order for Replay

When replaying the transactions on the target, you do not have to mirror the database connection environment on the target to achieve data integrity. As concurrent transactions are isolated from each other, you can execute the transactions on the target sequentially instead. Thus, you can use a single database connection to replay all transactions of the current transmission. However, you must execute the individual transactions in the correct sequence, which is given by the time of their completion on the source.

The following example shows why the transactions must be ordered by their completion time, not their start time.

Two tables are written by two concurrent transactions. Figure 3.24 shows how both transactions are running in parallel.

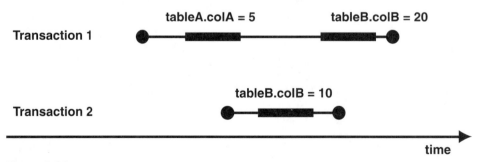

Figure 3.24
Two concurrent transactions

Transaction 1 starts first and updates tableA. Then Transaction 2 starts, updates tableB, and completes with a commit. Finally, Transaction 1 also updates tableB. After both transactions, colB of tableB has a value of 20.

If the ordering were done on the transaction start time, the update of Transaction 2 would be the last one. Thus, colB of tableB would have a value of 10 at the end, instead of 20. However, if the ordering is done on the end time of each transaction, colB of tableB has a value of 20 at the end, which is the correct value.

If Transaction 1 had written tableB before Transaction 2 (for example, instead of tableA), then Transaction 2 would have been blocked until the end of Transaction 1. Transaction 2 would have been executed after Transaction 1, and colB of tableB would have a value of 10. Here again the transactions have to be ordered on their completion, which produces the correct result.

A sufficiently precise timestamp is needed to distinguish the completion time of any two transactions and thereby correctly order the transactions.

Handling Triggers, If the Write Uses Standard SQL

Triggers are schema objects that perform additional operations on behalf of an initial operation. Triggered operations are also part of the initiating transaction and are logged in the same way as any other operation.

There is an issue around how the RDBMS behaves when logged changes get applied to the target database. If you can apply the log information to the target without ever triggering a secondary operation, then you are fine. But if a trigger could be fired by applying a log record, then you have to be concerned.

This applies to either triggers that match source ones, or totally different triggers at the target.

For example, a source table has a trigger that is fired on every UPDATE. This would INSERT the old state of the row into a history table. There is a similar trigger on the target table. An UPDATE of the row in the source log is recorded, and the triggered INSERT into the history table is also recorded as part of the transaction. When executing this transaction on the target, the UPDATE of the table is performed first. This fires the trigger on the target, which causes an entry into the history table. But the source also recorded an INSERT into the history table. When replaying the next operation, a second INSERT into the history table is performed. Thus, the history table would have two new entries instead of one.

Hence, if you don't take special precaution around the handling of triggers, you might perform more operations on the target than you performed on the source.

To solve the problem, you must eliminate the effect of the trigger on the target during transmissions. To achieve this, the replication link should connect to the target database with a dedicated user or a dedicated role that is only used for transmissions, but not by any other applications. Additionally, the trigger has to be defined in a manner (depending on the SQL dialect of the RDBMS) that does not perform any operations if the database connection uses this special user or role.

Prerequisites

This pattern depends on two features that the DBMS must provide and on a prerequisite for the data model:

- **A fine-grained clock.** The order in which transactions are executed on the source must be the same as the order in which they are replayed on the target. Thus, the clock must provide a sufficiently fine resolution to preserve the order. A clock grain of a millisecond is generally sufficient; many systems provide even microseconds. A clock with a resolution of whole seconds only will definitely prevent the use of this pattern.

- **Transaction Identifiers.** The RDBMS must provide a means to identify the operations that belonging to the same transaction. This is called a *Transaction Identifier* throughout the remaining discussion. It can be an opaque data type, and is generally provided to handle distributed transactions.

- **Unique key.** All tables of the replication set must have either unique keys or another combination of columns that uniquely identifies every row. The unique identifier of every row is referred to as the *Replication Key* throughout this document. After the Manipulate process, the resulting Replication Key must also identify every row in the target uniquely.

Elements of the Replication Building Block

The following paragraphs describe the elements of the replication building block for this type of replication.

Source

The source contains the replication set, which is a log of all changes that you want to acquire.

Acquire

The steps of Acquire are:

1. Connect to the source.
2. Find the transaction pending for transmission to the target that has the oldest completion timestamp.
3. Find the first operation of this transaction.
4. Pass the Transaction Identifier, the table name, the type of operation (INSERT, UPDATE, or DELETE) and the names and values of the columns to Manipulate.
5. Continue with step 4 until all operations for the current transaction are read.
6. Delete the record of the transmitted transaction, unless it is needed for other replication links.
7. Continue with step 2 until all transactions are read.

Manipulate

This service performs the following steps:

1. Get the first row from Acquire.

2. If the table needs some manipulation, perform the appropriate action, such as converting data types, and combining or splitting fields of the row.

3. Pass the Transaction Identifier, the table name, the type of operation (INSERT, UPDATE, or DELETE) and the names and values of the columns to the Write service.

4. Get the next row from Acquire and continue with step 2 until all rows are processed.

Write

The Write service performs the following steps:

1. Get the first row from Manipulate.

2. If the Transaction Identifier differs from the Transaction Identifier of the previously handled row, COMMIT the transaction.

3. Depending on the remaining attributes, build a SQL statement that INSERTs, UPDATEs, or DELETEs a single row in the target.

4. Get the next row from the Manipulate service and continue with step 2 until all rows are processed.

Target

The target is the database where the transactions are replayed. You must ensure that no triggered operations are executed, as described above.

Example

The *Implementing Master-Slave Transactional Incremental Replication Using SQL Server* pattern presents an implementation of the design pattern by the means provided with Microsoft® SQL Server™.

Resulting Context

The use of this pattern inherits the benefits and liabilities from *Master-Slave Replication* and has the following additional benefit and liability:

Benefit

- **Basis for other useful services.** Other services might have a similar need to use transactional information. For example, spin off the transmission data to a historical store, such as a data warehouse.

Liability

- **Dependencies of schemas.** This pattern depends greatly on the similarity between the source and the target schemas. If one of them changes, the other must change accordingly. (For minor changes, it could be sufficient to adapt Manipulate for the data conversion from the source schema to the target schema.)

Security Considerations

The database connection used to replay the transactions on the target must have sufficient access rights to INSERT, UPDATE, or DELETE in all tables belonging to the replication set. In addition, the Acquire database connection account needs to have SELECT or READ privileges on the source transaction objects.

It is recommended that you create a dedicated user in the target database with appropriate privileges and use this user for all transmissions. In general, this user will not be used for any other purposes.

Defining such a user allows you to tailor the privileges to the specific needs of Acquire or Write.

Operational Considerations

Before implementing *Master-Slave Transactional Incremental Replication*, the following are considerations to achieve smooth running operations:

- **Load on the source database server.** When a large number of targets want to use the same source for their replication links, then the source can have operational difficulties in meeting all their demands. In this case, consider using the *Master-Slave Cascading Replication* pattern.

- **Load on the target database server.** Transmissions replay transactions in the same way they were executed on the source. Although the transactions are executed sequentially on the target, the transmission consumes significant resources, such as CPU time and I/O activity, on the target. This impacts the response times of the applications during transmissions.

- **Space requirements for replaying the transactions on the target.** Every transaction on the source is replayed as a single transaction on the target. Thus, you must provide sufficient space in the logging system to complete the largest transaction that might be executed on the source. Although the source must deal with concurrent transactions that the target does not need, a good starting point is to configure the logging system of the target in the same way that it is configured on the source.

Variants

After introducing the solution for transmitting the changes of a replication set from the source to the target, two variants show possible enhancements. The first variant shows a way to obtain a higher robustness of the replication. The second one sketches the implementation of a change history.

Higher Robustness

When writing the transactions to the target, you might consider converting INSERTs into UPDATEs or vice versa. Thus, if an INSERT raises a duplicate key error, you perform an UPDATE instead; and if the number of rows being hit by an UPDATE is zero, you perform an INSERT instead. This is sometimes referred to as an UPSERT.

Although such error handling is not necessary as long as the content of the target corresponds exactly to the state of the source before the transaction, it offers a higher degree of robustness. If the content of the target had been changed, for example, by an erroneous action of an operation or administrator, the normal execution of the transaction would fail; however, such an error handling will again align the contents of the source and the target.

Implementing a Change History

Instead of updating changed rows, they can be appended by adding a version number. Therefore, the previous version of the target row will be kept to retain a change history at the target. For example, this information can be used to trace a stock's performance record.

Additional Prerequisites

Some preparations have to be made for this variant to work.

- The data schema must be extended by a version column.
- The version number must be managed by Write, which increases the version number before it writes the new row by performing an INSERT.

Operational Considerations

Because rows will not be updated but inserted, the target database grows faster than the source database. Therefore, you must provide an appropriate amount of free disk space at the target site.

Related Patterns

For more information, see the following related patterns:

Patterns That May Have Led You Here

- *Move Copy of Data.* This is the root pattern of this cluster; it presents the overall architecture for maintain copies of data after they have been updated.
- *Data Replication.* This pattern presents the architecture of a replication.
- *Master-Slave Replication.* This pattern describes design considerations for transmitting data from the source to the target by overwriting potential changes in the target on a higher level.
- *Capture Transaction Details.* This pattern describes the underlying change-capture service to provide transactional information from the source when a DBMS log is not available or is not to be used for this purpose.

Patterns That You Can Use Next

- *Implementing Master-Slave Transactional Incremental Replication Using SQL Server.* This pattern shows how to implement Master-Slave Transactional Incremental Replication by using SQL Server.

Other Patterns of Interest

- *Master-Slave Snapshot Replication.* This pattern presents a design for transmitting a complete replication set. This can be used to equalize both databases as a starting point before establishing an Incremental Replication.
- *Master-Slave Cascading Replication.* This pattern shows replication topologies where *Master-Slave Transactional Incremental Replication* can be used to design the individual replication links of the topology.

Implementing Master-Master Row-Level Synchronization Using SQL Server

Context

You want to build a master-master synchronization between two Microsoft® SQL Server™ databases, and you want to take advantage of the integrated synchronization functionality of SQL Server. The replication sets of the source and target are identical and manipulations of them are not intended. You want to detect and resolve potential conflicts at the row level. In addition, you want to be able to define the conflict resolution method according to your business needs (for example, the more recent change wins).

Note: This pattern uses terms and concepts introduced in the following patterns:

- *Move Copy of Data*
- *Data Replication*
- *Master-Master Replication*
- *Master-Master Row-Level Synchronization*

Background

Before introducing the implementation with SQL Server, this pattern covers the following topics:

- A summary of the synchronization building block as described in the *Master-Master Row-Level Synchronization* pattern
- The SQL Server replication services that this pattern uses (SQL Server merge replication).
- The mapping of the elements of the synchronization building block to the services of SQL Server.

Synchronization Building Block

The *Master-Master Row-Level Synchronization* design pattern uses a synchronization building block, which consists of two related replication links and a synchronization controller. Figure 3.25 on the next page shows *Master-Master Row-Level Synchronization* at the design level with the related replication links.

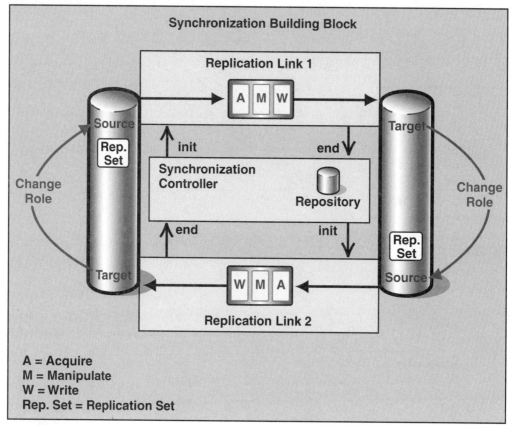

Figure 3.25
Master-Master Row-Level Synchronization at the design level

Synchronization Controller

The synchronization controller manages the synchronization. It relates both replication links and controls their invocations. The controller uses its own repository to store information about the synchronization, for example the time of the last synchronization for the replication link pair.

Source

The source contains the replication set, which is the data to be copied from the source and sent across a data movement link to the target.

Acquire

In the *Master-Master Row-Level Synchronization* pattern, the controller invokes the Acquire service. The Acquire service reads the data changes to be transmitted.

Manipulate

The Manipulate service performs simple data transformations, such as data type conversions and splitting or combining columns.

Write

The Write service updates the target with the manipulated rows. Before writing the updates, the Write service uses conflict detection and resolution methods to merge any data modifications that occurred after the last synchronization on both source and target.

Target

The Target is the database where the replication set is to be written.

SQL Server Replication Services

This section describes the types of replication available in SQL Server and the replication components used in this pattern.

Replication Types

SQL Server offers two types of replication that cope with updates to both source and target:

- **Transactional replication.** Conflicts are detected at the transaction level. If the transactions do not conflict with each other, changes are transmitted in both directions. However, if a conflict is detected, either the source or the target always wins; you cannot use any other conflict resolution methods with this type of replication.

- **Merge replication.** Conflicts can be detected at the row level or column level, but conflicts are always resolved at the row level. You can use different kinds of conflict resolutions methods with this type of replication. The data structure of the replication set on source and target must be identical.

Note: This pattern uses merge replication because it provides the ability to detect conflicts at the row level or column level and to define conflict resolution methods at the row level.

SQL Server merge replication uses several standard services to synchronize data between the publication database and the subscription database. Figure 3.26 on the next page shows the services and processes involved in such a transmission.

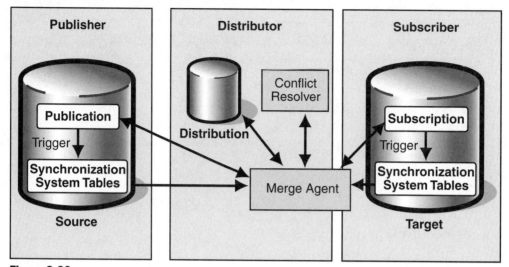

Figure 3.26
SQL Server merge replication

Platform Roles

SQL Server defines three roles for the platforms that are involved in synchronization:

- **Publisher.** The Publisher contains the source and defines the replication set (publication) to be replicated.
- **Distributor.** The Distributor holds the distribution database and the conflict resolver. It runs the cleanup jobs for managing the distribution database, and in a push replication also runs the Merge Agent. (The next section discusses these software components in detail.)
- **Subscriber.** The Subscriber contains the target and creates a subscription to subscribe a publication. In a pull replication, the Subscriber runs the Merge Agent.

The Distributor does not necessarily need to be a separate platform. Its role can also be assigned to the Publisher, where it is called a local Distributor. Otherwise it is called a remote Distributor.

Software Components

SQL Server replication contains the following software components:

- **Trigger.** In the source and the target, the configuration process creates system tables and triggers. The triggers track the changes on the replication sets and write them to the system tables.
- **Merge Agent.** The Merge Agent applies the initial snapshot to the Subscriber and moves and reconciles the data changes that occur to the replication set. Each merge subscription has its own Merge Agent that connects to both the Publisher

and the Subscriber and updates both. The Merge Agent runs at either the Distributor for push subscriptions or the Subscriber for pull subscriptions.

Note: The Merge Agent may serve several Subscribers, but this pattern considers only a single Subscriber.

In a merge replication with row-level conflict detection, there are three alternatives for the data flow:

- **Upload.** The changes are merged only in the target.
- **Download.** Only the source gets the merged data.
- **Bidirectional.** The replication first performs an upload (to merge at the target) and then after applying these changes performs a download (to merge at the original source).

Note: The Synchronization implementation pattern requires bidirectional transmission.

During synchronization, each changed row from the source is compared with the corresponding row from the target (Upload). If both rows have changed, there is a conflict. The merge agent uses the defined conflict resolver to choose a winning row. After finishing all source rows, the same process starts with all changed target rows (Download).

- **Conflict resolver.** The conflict resolver is used to choose a winning row if a conflict occurs. SQL Server provides a default priority-based conflict resolver and a number of custom conflict resolvers. You can also write custom conflict resolvers. SQL Server 2000 includes the following custom resolvers:
  - Additive Conflict Resolver
  - Averaging Conflict Resolver
  - DATETIME (Earlier Wins) Conflict Resolver
  - DATETIME (Later Wins) Conflict Resolver
  - Maximum Conflict Resolver
  - Merge Text Conflict Resolver
  - Minimum Conflict Resolver
  - Subscriber Always Wins Conflict Resolver
  - Priority Column Resolver
  - Upload Only Conflict Resolver
  - Download Only Conflict Resolver
  - Stored Procedure

Alternatively, you can use a user-written conflict resolver, which is implemented as stored procedures, or a COM conflict resolver.

- **Distribution database.** This additional database is needed to store the metadata, the history, and the error log of the replication process. The distribution database must be a SQL Server database and is located on either the publisher (called a local Distributor) or on a dedicated platform (called a remote Distributor).
- **Cleanup jobs.** Independent of the transmission process, cleanup jobs run on the distribution database and perform the following tasks:
  - **Agent History Clean Up: Distribution.** Removes replication agent history from the distribution database.
  - **Distribution Clean Up: Distribution.** Removes replicated transactions from the distribution database.
  - **Expired Subscription Clean Up.** Detects and removes expired subscriptions from publication databases.
  - **Reinitialize Subscriptions Having Data Validation Failures.** Reinitializes all subscriptions that have data validation failures.
  - **Replication Agents Checkup.** Detects replication agents that are not actively logging history.

Mapping the Synchronization Building Block to SQL Server

Figure 3.27 shows how the elements of the synchronization building block map to those of SQL Server merge replication.

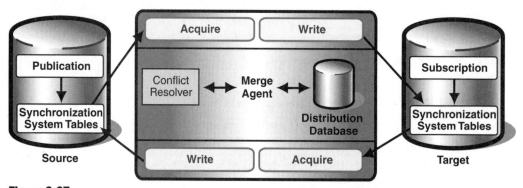

Figure 3.27
SQL Server implementation of Master-Master Row-Level Synchronization design

Defining the Replication Set

The replication set that is to be synchronized between the source and the target in SQL Server is called a publication on the Publisher and a subscription on the Subscriber. The elements of a subscription are identical to those of a publication. This kind of publication consists of one or more tables, or only parts of tables. The parts of tables can be defined in one or two ways by:

- Filtering the rows to be replicated by defining a search condition.

  In the theory of relational databases, the result is called a restriction.

- Filtering the columns to be replicated as a subset of the table's columns.

  In the theory of relational databases, the result is called a projection.

Synchronization Controller

In the SQL-Server environment, the Merge Agent takes the role of the synchronization controller. The Merge Agent executes Replication Link 1 to upload changes from the Publisher, and then executes Replication Link 2 to download the Subscriber updates.

Source

The source is the publication database, which contains the publication to be replicated and the synchronization system tables.

Acquire

The changes on the replication set are tracked by triggers and are written to local system tables. These changes are then acquired by the Merge Agent.

Manipulate

In a merge replication environment, data manipulations within the transmission are not permitted.

Write

The replication set is written to the target by the Merge Agent, which detects and resolves conflicts before it writes the data.

Target

The target is the Subscription database, which contains the corresponding replication set to the source.

Implementation Strategy

The schemas of the publications in both Publisher and Subscriber must be identical. SQL Server merge replication does not support any manipulations during transmissions.

▶ **To set up a new replication link**

1. Configure the Distributor:
   a. Create the distribution database: This is an internal SQL Server database used from the Distributor. In most cases, you use the default options to create this database, but you can also customize it.

   b. Choose the snapshot folder: You can either choose the default folder for exchanging the initial snapshot files or you use a custom folder.

   c. Set up the Subscriber parameter: To define the default parameter for all subscribers, you can confirm the offered configuration options or customize them.

2. Define the publication:

   a. For each table, decide whether to use the default conflict resolver provided or use a custom resolver.

   b. If you want to use a custom Conflict Resolver that has additional requirements, it may be necessary to modify the table (for example, add a timestamp column for the DATETIME Conflict Resolver and create triggers to update it).

   c. Select the publication database that includes the replication set.

   d. Select the possible database systems that the Subscribers will use: SQL Server 2000 or earlier versions of SQL Server.

   e. Select the tables to be replicated; for each table, specify a conflict detection method and a Conflict Resolver.

   f. For each table, specify whether the entire table should be replicated, or restrict the table by specifying horizontal and vertical filters.

   g. Decide whether anonymous Subscribers are allowed to subscribe to the publication.

   h. Decide how often the Snapshot Agent creates new snapshots.

3. Define the subscription:

   a. Decide if you want a pull or a push subscription.

   b. Select the publication you want to subscribe to.

   c. Choose the subscription database.

   d. Decide whether to initialize the subscriber using an initial snapshot from the publisher or whether to populate the database manually.

   e. If you want to start the transmission automatically, define a schedule.

   f. Verify that the SQL Server Agent is running at the Publisher, the Distributor, and all Subscribers.

At this point, all elements of the replication link have been configured. From now on, both Publisher and Subscriber will log all changes to the specified replication set using triggers.

The SQL Server merge replication runs different jobs:

- Snapshot Agent: Creates the initial snapshot on the Publisher.
- Merge Agent: Applies the initial snapshot on the subscription database. Merges the changes from publication database and subscription database, and detects and resolve conflicts using the chosen Conflict Resolver.
- Cleanup jobs: Clean up the Distribution Database on the Distributor.

The example that follows describes in detail how to use the SQL Server wizards to set up this kind of replication link.

Example

This example describes a synchronization performed with SQL Server merge replication. The synchronization uses a table from the Pubs sample database, which is delivered with SQL Server.

Overview

This example uses two computers to demonstrate the synchronization. One computer, PUB_SERVER, hosts the Publisher, including the database PUB_DB, and a local Distributor, including the default Distribution database, Distribution. Another computer, SUBS_SERVER, forms the subscriber and has a database identical to PUB_DB named SUBS_DB. An initial snapshot is used to transmit the data schema and populate the tables on the Subscription database. Figure 3.28 shows the architecture of the example.

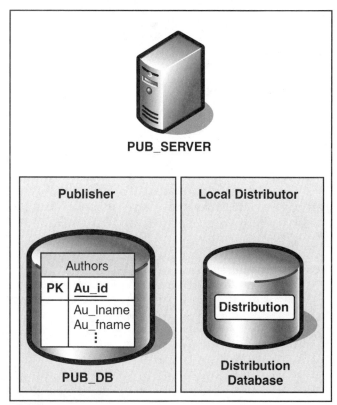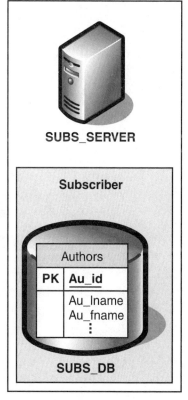

Figure 3.28
Example environment

The conflict resolution mechanism used is an integrated custom Microsoft SQL Server DATETIME (Earlier Wins) Conflict Resolver. Each table in the replication set therefore needs a special column of type DATETIME. This column must be updated each time a row is modified. The following triggers perform this task:

```
CREATE TRIGGER authors_inserted ON dbo.authors
AFTER INSERT, UPDATE
AS
UPDATE dbo.authors
SET last_changed = getdate()
WHERE au_id = inserted.au_id;

CREATE TRIGGER authors_deleted ON dbo.authors
BEFORE DELETE
AS
UPDATE dbo.authors
SET last_changed = getdate()
WHERE au_id = deleted.au_id;
```

The triggers were created on the Subscription database when the initial snapshot was applied. If you don't use an initial snapshot, you have to create the triggers yourself that correspond to the Publication database. The subscriber initiates the synchronization process every 15 minutes. Publication and Subscription have identical data structures.

Configuring the Publisher and the Distributor

To set up the example environment, follow these steps in the Configure Publishing and Distribution Wizard.

1. In SQL Server Enterprise Manager, select the publication database server, right-click **Replication**, and then click **Configure Publishing, Subscribers and Distribution**.

2. On the **Select Distributor** page, select **Make *Pub_Server* its own Distributor**, where *Pub_Server* is the name of the server you want to configure as a Distributor. Click **Next**.

Note: The distributor can be located on the same server as the Publisher, in which case it is called a local distributor, or on a remote server. This example uses a local Distributor.

---

3. On the **Specify Snapshot Folder** page, type the name of a shared folder on the Distributor where the Snapshot Agent can store snapshot files.

> **Note:** You must create and share this folder manually or use an existing system shared folder for this purpose. You should use a manually defined snapshot folder because the default uses a system internal share, such as C$. These shares are used for administrative purposes.

4. On the **Customize the Configuration** page, select **No, use the following default settings** to create a default distribution database.

> **Note:** In this simple example, it's sufficient to use the default settings. In a more complex environment, you should manually configure the distribution database.

Creating a Publication

Next, use the Create Publication Wizard to create a publication on the Publisher.

1. In SQL Server Enterprise Manager, select the publication database server, expand **Replication,** right-click **Publications**, and then click **New Publication**.

2. On the **Welcome Screen**, click **Next**.

3. On the **Choose Publication Database** page, select *Pub_DB* as the Publication Database, where *Pub_DB* is the name of your publication database for the replication.

4. On the **Select Publication Type** page, select **Merge Publication** to create a publication for the synchronization.

5. On the **Specify Subscriber Types** page, select only **Servers running SQL Server 2000.**

6. The **Specify Articles** page shows possible objects for replication in the Publication Database. From the **Object Type Tables** list, select the **authors** table. Click the ellipses (...) button to specify the properties for this article.

7. On the **Table Article Properties** page, specify the type of conflict detection and select a resolver:

   a. Click the **General** tab and select **Treat changes to the same row as a conflict** to enable conflict detection.

   b. On the **Resolver** tab, click **Use this custom resolver** and select **Microsoft SQL Server DATETIME (Earlier Wins) Conflict Resolver**. In the text box, specify the DATETIME column used by the resolver. In this case, the column is named **last_changed**.

Figure 3.29 on the next page shows the **General** and **Resolver** tabs of the **Table Articles Properties** page.

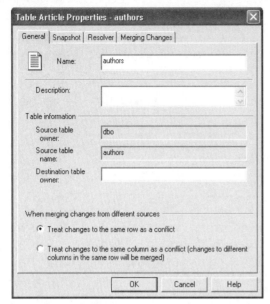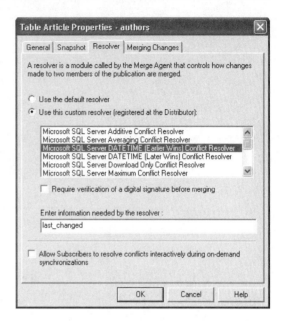

Figure 3.29
Tabs on the Table Articles Properties page

8. The **Article Issues** page informs you that each table of the publication needs a unique identifier column with the data type ROWGUIDCOL. If this column does not exist, it is created automatically. Click **Next** to proceed.

9. On the **Select Publication Name and Description** page, specify the **Publication name** as **example**. The default entry for the publication description can be used.

10. On the **Customize the Properties of the Publication** page, select the option beginning with **No, create the publication as specified** to accept the default options shown in the text box below the options.

11. On the **Completing the Create Publication Wizard** page, click **Finish** to create the publication.

Creating a Subscription

To complete the configuration, use the Pull Subscription Wizard to create a pull subscription for the defined publication on the Subscriber.

1. In SQL Server Enterprise Manager, select the subscription database server, open **Replication,** right-click **Subscriptions**, and then click **New Pull Subscription**.

2. On the **Welcome Screen**, click **Next**.

3. On the **Look for Publications** page, select **Look at publications from registered servers**.

4. On the **Choose Publication** page, expand **Pub_Server** and select the Publication named **example:pub_db**, where *Pub_Server* is the name of your Publisher and *example:pub_db* is the name of your publication (see Figure 3.30).

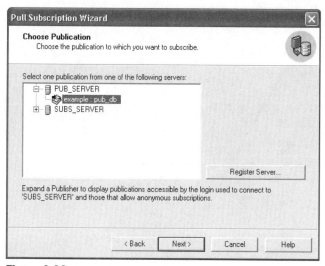

Figure 3.30
Choose Publication page

5. On the **Specify Synchronization Agent Login** page, select **Use SQL Server Authentication**. Enter the login and the password of a user account that is used to connect to the Publisher during the replication.

6. On the **Choose Destination Database** page, select **Subs_DB** as the database for the Subscription, where *Subs_DB* is the name of your subscription database.

7. On the **Initialize Subscription** page, select **Yes, initialize the schema and the data**, and then click **Start the Merge Agent to initialize the Subscription immediately** to use a snapshot from the Publication database to create an identical author table on the Subscription database.

8. On the **Snapshot Delivery** page, specify the snapshot folder. This example uses the default folder of the publication.

9. On the **Set Distribution Agent Schedule** page, select **Using the following schedule**, and then click **Change** to specify a new schedule for the Distribution Agent.

10. On the **Edit Recurring Job Schedule** page, under **Occurs**, select **Daily**. Under **Daily Frequency**, select **Occurs every** and specify an interval of 15 minutes. (See Figure 3.31 on the next page.)

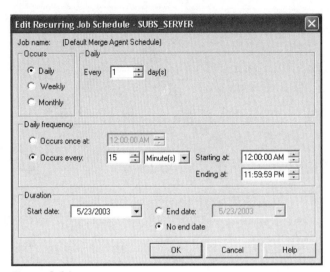

Figure 3.31
Edit Recurring Job Schedule page

11. On the **Set Subscription Priority** page, select **Use the Publisher as a proxy** (the example does not use a priority-based conflict resolver).

12. The **Start Required Services** page shows the status of the SQL Server Agent on the Subscriber. If the SQL Server Agent is not running, select the check box next to the entry for the Agent. The Agent will start after the wizard creates the subscription.

13. On the **Completing the Pull Subscription Wizard** page, review the options for the specified subscription. Click **Finish** to create the subscription with these options.

The configuration process is finished. During this process, the system tables and triggers for the merge replication are installed on the Publisher and the Subscriber. The initial snapshot is applied, and now every change on the replication set is logged in both databases.

Before starting the first transmission, you should check the following:

- Make sure that the Snapshot Agent has created the first initial snapshot. You may need to start the Snapshot Agent manually on the publication database.

- Make sure that the Merge Agent has initialized the schema. If this has not been done automatically, you can start the process manually on the subscription database.

- Ensure that each replication agent is able to communicate with all servers involved in the replication topology. You can do so by logging on to the required server and database using SQL Query Analyzer or the SQL Server command line utility called osql.

Starting and Restarting the Synchronization

To start the synchronization manually, follow these steps:

1. In SQL Server Enterprise Manager, select the publication database server, open **Replication Monitor,** select **Publishers**, **Pub_Server**, and open the publication **example:pub_db**.

2. Right-click **Snapshot Agent** and select **Start Agent** to create an initial snapshot.

3. Right-click **SUBS_Server:subs_db** and select **Start Synchronizing** to start the synchronization.

The replication usually runs on a defined schedule. If you want to test the replication or start the merge replication immediately, however, you need to start the replication manually.

Testing the Example

You can easily test the functionality of the implemented synchronization by changing data in the publication database and the subscription database, starting the synchronization, and checking to see if the corresponding data has changed accordingly.

To check various kinds of data changes, perform INSERT, UPDATE, and DELETE operations on the publication database and the subscription database. The updates should involve the same rows in both databases. Manipulate the data so that different conflicts occur and so that both databases include winning rows, as follows:

1. Change a row in the publication database. For example:

```
UPDATE authors SET au_lname = 'Smith' WHERE au_id = '807-91-6654'

INSERT INTO authors (au_id, au_lname, au_fname, phone, contract)
       VALUES ('453102-3255', 'Berg', 'Karen', '400 486-234', 1)

DELETE FROM authors WHERE au_id = '672-71-3249'
```

2. Change the corresponding row in the subscription database so that a conflict occurs. For example:

```
UPDATE authors SET au_lname = 'Meyer' WHERE author_id = '807-91-6654'
```

3. Start the synchronization manually.

4. Check to see if the rows changed in both databases. Verify that the expected column won the conflict that occurred during the transmission. For example:

```
SELECT * FROM authors
```

5. Check the history of the subscription in the replication monitor to make sure that the conflict was logged as detected and resolved.

Resulting Context

The implementation described in this pattern detects and resolves conflicts at the row level. Updates on different columns of the same row are treated as conflicts, and only the source changes or the target changes will remain after a transmission.

The implementation of the *Master-Master Row-Level Synchronization* pattern has the same benefits and liabilities as the design pattern. In addition, the use of this pattern results in the following benefits and liabilities:

Benefits

- **Integrated into SQL Server Enterpise Manager.** The configuration and execution of a replication in SQL Server is integrated into SQL Server administration and can be easily done with the SQL Server Enterprise Manager.

Liabilities

- **Additional database to be managed.** The implementation requires the distribution database as an additional database that must also be managed.

Testing Considerations

After you set up the merge replication as described in this pattern, you must test it thoroughly. Your test cases should cover these scenarios and others:

- Correct transmission of changes to the publication.
- Correct conflict resolution in terms of the right row winning during a conflict.
- The longest disconnection between the publication database and the Subscription database that you expect under production conditions.
- Network interruption between the publication database and the distribution database during updates on the publication database.
- Network interruption between the distribution database and the subscription database during a running transmission.
- A hard abort of database system on the Subscription database during a running transmission.

After each test, make sure that the data at both ends of the replication is consistent.

Finally, put the highest expected load on both the publication database and the subscription database and check to see if the synchronization still runs correctly.

Security Considerations

To secure the connection between the Distributor and the Subscribers, do one of the following:

- Use a SQL Server user account to connect to the Distributor.

- Place all computers in one Windows domain, or have a common user with the same password on all computers. Then use a trusted Windows connection between Distributor and Subscribers.

If you prefer a security approach that is independent of the operating system, you should use SQL Server authentication.

Note: The SQL Server Agents on all systems must run on a local or a domain account, not on the LocalSystem account. Otherwise, the replication will not work.

Operational Considerations

The SQL Server Agent manages the different jobs of the replication. Schedules for these jobs were defined during the configuration. Additionally, you can start each job manually using the SQL Server Enterprise Manager.

The Replication Monitor in SQL Server Enterprise Manager provides the following information:

- A list of all publications and attached agents with the time and the duration of the last execution and information about the last action.
- A list of all agents grouped by task with current status and a history of actions.
- The event log entries created by Replication Alerts, which monitor the replication process.

If the replication fails, do the following:

- Check to see if the accounts have network access rights.
- Check the history of the subscription to determine the reason that synchronization failed.
- Check the Replication Monitor for highlighted replication failures.

Related Patterns

For more information, see the following related patterns.

Patterns That May Have Led You Here

- *Move Copy of Data.* This pattern is the root pattern of this cluster. It presents the fundamental data movement building block consisting of source, data movement set, data movement link, and target. In such a block, transmissions are done asynchronously (or some time after the update of the source). Thus, the target applications must tolerate a period of latency until changes are delivered.
- *Data Replication.* This pattern presents the overall architecture of replication.

- *Master-Master Replication*. This pattern presents the general design of a replication that accepts updates by applications on both source and target, and exchanges the changes in both directions.

- *Master-Master Row-Level Synchronization*. This pattern presents the design of synchronization.

Other Patterns of Interest

- *Implementing Master-Slave Snapshot Replication Using SQL Server*. This pattern describes the implementation of a snapshot replication, which is used as a starting point when setting up a synchronization.

- *Capture Transaction Details*. This pattern gives background information about using triggers to record changes.

Implementing Master-Slave Snapshot Replication Using SQL Server

Context

You want to implement the design pattern *Master-Slave Snapshot Replication*. You are replicating between two Microsoft® SQL Server™ databases, and you want to take advantage of the integrated functionality of SQL Server. The replication set consists of entire rows, not just changes that have occurred to rows since the last replication. Any changes to the replication data at the target that may have occurred since the last transmission will be overwritten by a new transmission.

Note: This pattern uses terms and concepts introduced in the following patterns:

- *Move Copy of Data*
- *Data Replication*
- *Master-Slave Replication*
- *Master-Slave Snapshot Replication*

Background

Before introducing the implementation with SQL Server, this pattern covers the following topics:

- A summary of the replication building block as described in the *Master-Slave Replication* pattern
- The SQL Server replication services that this pattern uses (SQL Server snapshot replication)
- The mapping of the elements of the replication building block to the services of SQL Server

Replication Building Block

The replication building block used in the *Master-Slave Snapshot Replication* pattern consists of a source and a target that are connected by a replication link, as Figure 3.32 on the next page shows.

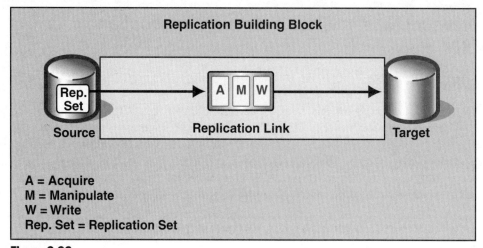

Figure 3.32
Replication building block for Master-Slave Snapshot Replication

Source

The source contains the replication set, which is the data to be copied from the source and sent across a data movement link to the target.

Acquire

The Acquire service reads the rows to be replicated.

Manipulate

The Manipulate service performs simple data transformations, such as data type conversions and splitting or combining columns.

Write

The Write service updates the target with the manipulated rows.

Target

The target is the database where the replication set is to be written.

Moving the replication set from source to target according to defined functional and operational requirements is called a transmission.

SQL Server Snapshot Replication

SQL Server replication uses several standard services to move data from a publication database to a subscription database. Figure 3.33 shows the services and processes involved in SQL Server snapshot replication.

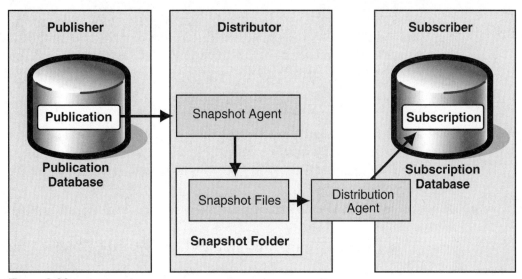

Figure 3.33
SQL Server snapshot replication

Platform Roles

SQL Server defines three roles for the platforms involved in the replication:

- **Publisher.** The Publisher contains the source. In this environment, the Subscriber defines the replication set (publication) to be replicated.

- **Distributor.** The Distributor holds a distribution database that is used for storing replication metadata. The Snapshot Agent runs on the Distributor and creates the snapshot files from the publication. In a push subscription, the Distributor also runs the Distribution Agent. Additionally, the cleanup jobs for managing the distribution database run here.

- **Subscriber.** The Subscriber contains the target and creates a subscription for the publication. In a pull subscription, the Subscriber runs the Distribution Agent.

The Distributor does not necessarily need to be a separate platform. Its role can also be assigned to the Publisher, where it is called a local Distributor. Otherwise, it is called a remote Distributor.

Software Components

SQL Server snapshot replication contains two processes:

- **Snapshot Agent.** The Snapshot Agent reads all the articles of a publication and writes the schema and data to a set of snapshot files. The snapshot files are stored in a shared snapshot folder. The folder is typically located on the Distributor, but in general it can be any shared folder that is accessible by both source and target.

- **Distribution Agent.** The Distribution Agent may run on the Subscriber (pull subscription), or it may run on the distributor (push subscription). The Distribution

Agent reads the snapshot file from the shared snapshot folder and writes its content to the target. Before actually writing the data, it can be manipulated by using a data transmission service (DTS) package that the Subscriber defines.

Note: The Distribution Agent may serve several Subscribers, but this pattern considers only a single Subscriber.

Independent of the replication processes, **cleanup jobs** run on the distribution database and perform the following tasks:

- **Agent History Clean Up: Distribution.** Removes replication agent history from the distribution database.
- **Distribution Clean Up: Distribution.** Removes replicated transactions from the distribution database.
- **Expired Subscription Clean Up.** Detects and removes expired subscriptions from publication databases.
- **Reinitialize Subscriptions Having Data Validation Failures.** Reinitializes all subscriptions that have data validation failures.
- **Replication Agents Checkup.** Detects replication agents that are not actively logging history.

Mapping the Replication Building Block to SQL Server

Figure 3.34 shows how the elements of the replication building block correspond to those of a SQL Server snapshot replication.

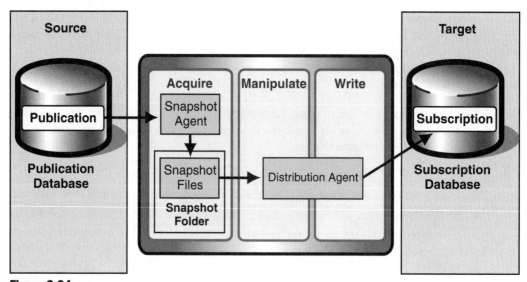

Figure 3.34
SQL Server implementation of the replication building block

Source

The source is the publication database that contains the publication to be replicated and takes on the role of the Publisher.

Replication Set

In SQL Server, the replication set to be transmitted from the Publisher to the Subscriber is called a publication. A publication consists of one or more tables, or only parts of tables. Parts of tables can be defined by:

- Filtering the rows to be replicated by defining a search condition.

  In the theory of relational databases, the result is called a restriction.

- Filtering the columns to be replicated as a subset of the table's columns.

  In the theory of relational databases, the result is called a projection.

Acquire

The Snapshot Agent reads all of the data from the defined publication into snapshot files and stores them in a shared snapshot folder.

Manipulate

The Distribution Agent can manipulate data before the data is written to the target. When the target registers its subscription to the Distributor, it can define a DTS package that the Distributor will call before sending the data to the Subscriber. Each Subscriber can use its own package; different Subscribers can get various views of the same data.

Within a DTS package, you can define any manipulations using the data of the current row and the possibilities of an ActiveX script language. Each row from the source can result in only one row at the target, or it can be skipped. Fields can be split or combined. Additionally, any kind of data type conversions and changes of field names can be done.

Write

The Distribution Agent writes the contents of the snapshot file to the target. The agent reads the snapshot file from the shared snapshot folder and applies the schema and the data to the target. Name conflicts during the write can be resolved in different ways. The default option in a snapshot replication is to drop the existing table and recreate it from the snapshot file. Another option is to leave the table on the target unchanged and reject the relevant data in the snapshot file. The last option is to delete the data on the target and use the empty table to write only the data from the snapshot file. In the case of using the existing table, the schema information from the snapshot file is not needed.

Target

The target is the subscription database, where the transmitted and possibly manipulated replication set is written. The target takes on the role of the Subscriber.

Implementation Strategy

To set up a new replication link, follow these steps:

1. Configure the Distributor:
    a. Create the distribution database. This is an internal SQL Server database used from the Distributor. In most cases, you use the default options to create this database, but you can also customize it.
    b. Choose the snapshot folder. You can either choose the default folder for exchanging the initial snapshot files or use a custom folder.
    c. Set up the Subscriber parameter: To define the default parameter for all Subscribers, you can confirm the offered configuration options or customize them.

2. Define the publication:
    a. Select the publication database that includes the publication.
    b. Decide if you want to transform the data during the transmission. If so, any Subscriber must have a DTS package for the transformation.
    c. Select the possible database systems the Subscribers will use: SQL Server 2000 or earlier versions of SQL Server.
    d. For each table, specify whether the entire table should be replicated, or restrict the table by specifying horizontal and vertical filters.
    e. Decide whether anonymous Subscribers are allowed to subscribe to the publication.
    f. Decide how often the Snapshot Agent creates new snapshots.

3. Create a DTS package for the transformation, if you have decided to use one.

4. Define the subscription:
    a. Decide if you want a pull or a push subscription.
    b. Select the publication you want to subscribe to.
    c. Choose the subscription database.
    d. If you want to start the transmission automatically, define a schedule.
    e. Specify the DTS package you want to use for this subscriber.
    f. Verify that all required services are started.

At this point, all elements of the replication link have been configured. From now on, both the publication database and the subscription database will log all changes to the specified replication set using triggers.

The SQL Server snapshot replication runs different jobs:

- Snapshot Agent: Creates the initial snapshot from the Publisher.
- Distribution Agent: Applies the snapshots on the Subscriber.
- Cleanup jobs: Clean up the distribution database on the Distributor.

The example that follows describes in detail how to use the SQL Server wizards to set up such a replication link.

Example

This example shows how to configure snapshot replication based on a particular replication set. The replication set used here is the authors table from the pubs sample database, which is delivered with SQL Server.

Overview

The environment has two SQL Server computers: PUB_SERVER and SUBS_SERVER. The Publisher has a database, PUB_DB, that contains the authors table from the pubs sample database. The Subscriber has an empty database, SUBS_DB. (See Figure 3.35.)

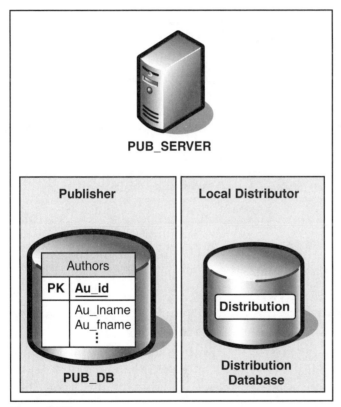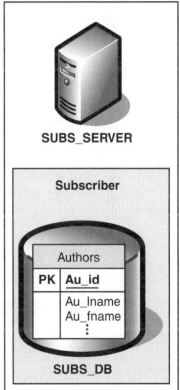

Figure 3.35
Example environment

The introduced configuration describes a snapshot replication using pull subscription where the Subscriber initiates the replication every two hours. The data from the Publisher will be manipulated during the replication. The first and the last name from the authors table will be converted to uppercase.

Configuring the Publisher and the Distributor

To set up the example environment, follow these steps in the Configure Publishing and Distribution Wizard.

1. In SQL Server Enterprise Manager, select the publication database server, right-click **Replication**, and then click **Configure Publishing, Subscribers and Distribution**.

2. On the **Select Distributor** page, select **Make *Pub_Server* its own Distributor**, where *Pub_Server* is the name of the server you want to configure as a Distributor. Click **Next**.

> **Note:** The Distributor can be located on the same server as the Publisher, in which case it is called a local Distributor, or on a remote server. This example uses a local Distributor.

3. On the **Specify Snapshot Folder** page, type the name of a shared folder on the Distributor where the Snapshot Agent can store snapshot files.

> **Note:** It is recommended that you use a manually defined snapshot folder because the default uses a system internal share, such as C$. These shares are used for administrative purposes.

4. On the **Customize the Configuration** page, select **No, use the following default settings** to create a default distribution database.

> **Note:** In this simple example, it is sufficient to use the default settings. In a more complex environment, you should manually configure the distribution database.

Creating a Publication

Next, use the Create Publication Wizard to create a publication on the Publisher.

1. In SQL Server Enterprise Manager, select the publication database server, expand **Replication**, right-click **Publications**, and then click **New Publication**.

2. On the **Welcome Screen**, check the **Show advanced options** check box to use this wizard with the advanced options needed to enable a transformation of the data.

3. On the **Choose Publication Database** page, select *Pub_DB* as the publication database, where *Pub_DB* is the name of your database for the replication.

4. On the **Select Publication Type** page, select **Snapshot Publication** to create a publication for a snapshot replication.

5. You do not want to allow the replication of changes from the subscriber to the publisher; therefore, ensure that no option is selected on the **Updateable Subscription** page.

6. On the **Transform Published Data** page, select **Yes, transform the data** to enable the transformation during the replication.

7. On the **Specify Subscriber Types** page, select only **Servers running SQL Server 2000**.

8. The **Specify Articles** page shows possible objects for replication in the publication database. From the **Object Type Tables** list, select the table **authors**.

Note: Clicking the ellipses (**...**) button for each object shows additional properties for the replication. You do not need them in this example.

---

9. On the **Select Publication Name and Description** page, specify the Publication name as **example**. The default publication description can be used.

10. On the **Customize the Properties of the Publication** page, select the option beginning with **Yes, I will define**, because you need a special schedule for the Snapshot Agent.

11. The **Filter Data** page allows you to specify filters for the data. Since this is not necessary in this example, click **Next**.

12. On the **Allow Anonymous Subscriptions** page, select **No, allow only named subscriptions** to prohibit anonymous access in this example.

Note: Anonymous subscriptions are pull subscriptions from Subscribers that are not registered on the Publisher. If you want to allow anonymous subscriptions, you must change this option.

---

13. On the **Set Snapshot Agent Schedule** page, click **Change** to specify a new schedule for the Snapshot Agent.

14. On the **Edit Recurring Job Schedule** page, define the schedule for the Snapshot Agent as a daily run with an interval of two hours. (See Figure 3.36 on the next page.)

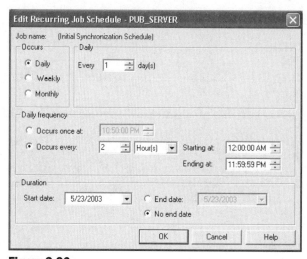

Figure 3.36
Edit Recurring Job Schedule page

15. On the **Completing the Create Publication Wizard** page, review the options for the specified publication. Click **Finish** to create the publication with these options.

Defining a DTS Package for the Transformation

Before you can create a subscription to the defined publication, you must create a DTS package for the transformation.

1. In SQL Server Enterprise Manager, select the publication database server, expand **Replication**, open **Publications**, right-click the **example:pub_db** replication, and then click **Properties**.

2. On the **Publication Properties** page, click the **Subscriptions** tab, and then click **Transformations**.

3. On the **Welcome Screen**, click **Next**.

4. On the **Choose a Destination** page, select the target server and database. (See Figure 3.37.)

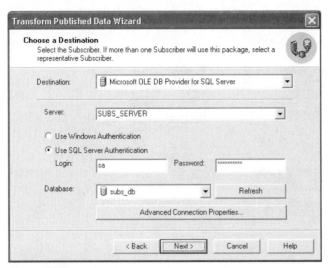

Figure 3.37
Choose a Destination page

5. On the **Define Transformations** page, click the ellipses (...) button from the article authors.

6. On the **Column Mappings** tab of the **Column Mappings and Transformations** page, select **Drop the existing table and recreate it** from the list box. Leave the mappings unchanged. (See Figure 3.38.)

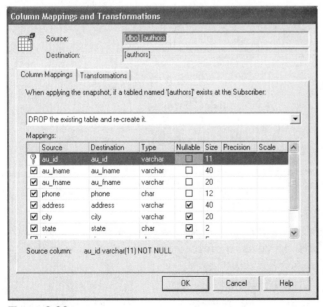

Figure 3.38
Column Mappings tab on the Column Mappings and Transformations page

7. Click the **Transformations** tab. Click **Transform data using the following script** and select **VB Script Language** from the list box. (See Figure 3.39.)

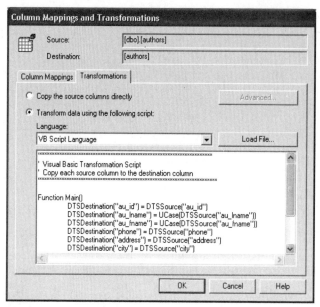

Figure 3.39

Transformations tab on the Column Mappings and Transformations page

8. Use the following code to transform the first and the last name of the author to uppercase:

```
Function Main()
    DTSDestination("au_id") = DTSSource("au_id")
    DTSDestination("au_lname") = UCase(DTSSource("au_lname"))
    DTSDestination("au_fname") = UCase(DTSSource("au_fname"))
    DTSDestination("phone") = DTSSource("phone")
    DTSDestination("address") = DTSSource("address")
    DTSDestination("city") = DTSSource("city")
    DTSDestination("state") = DTSSource("state")
    DTSDestination("zip") = DTSSource("zip")
    DTSDestination("contract") = DTSSource("contract")
    Main = DTSTransformStat_OK
End Function
```

9. On the **DTS Package Location** page, select the option to save the package on the Distributor. Use the SQL Server authentication option, and insert the user and the password to connect to the Distributor.

10. On the **DTS Package Identification** page, specify the name of the package. In this example, the name should be **transform_sub**. You do not need to define an owner password.

11. On the **Completing the Transform Published Data Wizard** page, click **Finish** to save the package as specified.

Creating a Subscription

To complete the configuration, you must create a pull subscription of the defined publication on the target.

1. In SQL Server Enterprise Manager, select the target database server, expand **Replication,** right-click **Subscriptions**, and then click **New Pull Subscription**.

2. On the **Welcome Screen,** click **Next**.

3. On the **Look for Publications** page, select **Look at publications from registered servers**.

4. On the **Choose Publication** page, expand **PUB_SERVER** and select the publication named **example:pub_db**, where *PUB_SERVER* is the name of your Publisher and *example:pub_db* is the name of your publication. (See Figure 3.40.)

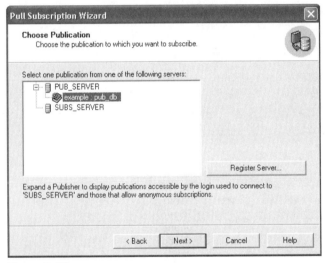

Figure 3.40
Choose Publication page

5. On the **Specify Synchronization Agent Login** page, select **Use SQL Server Authentication**. Enter the login and the password of a user account that is used to connect to the Publisher during the replication.

6. On the **Choose Destination Database** page, select **Subs_DB** as the database for the subscription, where *Subs_DB* is the name of your target database.

7. On the **Initialize Subscription** page, the option **Yes, initialize the schema and the data** cannot be changed because you use a snapshot replication.

8. On the **Snapshot Delivery** page, specify the snapshot folder. This example uses the default folder of the publication.

9. On the **Set Distribution Agent Schedule** page, select **Using the following schedule** and click **Change** to specify a new schedule for the Distribution Agent.

10. On the **Edit Recurring Job Schedule** page, define the schedule for the Distribution Agent as a daily run with an interval of two hours. (See Figure 3.41.)

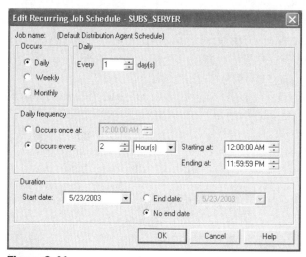

Figure 3.41
Edit Recurring Job Schedule page

11. On the **Specify DTS Package** page, select **Distributor** and click **List packages**. For the transformation, select the **transform_sub** package you created previously. (See Figure 3.42.)

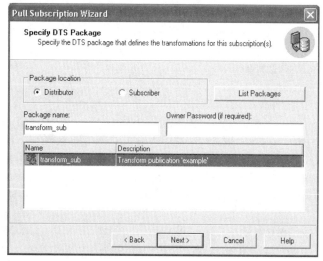

Figure 3.42
Specify DTS Package page

12. The **Start Required Services** page shows the status of the SQL Server Agent on the Subscriber. If the SQL Server Agent is not running, select the check box next to the entry for the agent. The agent will be started after the wizard creates the subscription.

13. On the **Completing the Pull Subscription Wizard** page, review the options for the specified subscription. Click **Finish** to create the subscription with these options.

Starting and Restarting the Snapshot Replication

To start or restart the snapshot replication manually for testing purposes, follow these steps:

1. In SQL Server Enterprise Manager, select the publication database server, open **Replication Monitor**, select **Publishers, Pub_Server**, and open the publication **example:pub_db**.

2. Right-click **Snapshot Agent** and click **Start Agent** to create an initial snapshot.

3. Right-click **SUBS_Server:subs_db** and select **Start Synchronizing** to start the replication.

The replication usually runs on a defined schedule. If you want to test the replication or start the snapshot replication immediately, however, you need to start the replication manually.

Testing the Example

You can easily test the functionality of the implemented snapshot replication by changing some data in the publication, starting the replication process, and checking to see if the subscription database has changed accordingly.

To check various kinds of data changes, perform INSERT, UPDATE, and DELETE operations on the data in the publication.

1. Change data in the publication. For example:

```
UPDATE authors SET au_lname = 'Smith' WHERE au_id = '807-91-6654'

INSERT INTO authors (au_id, au_lname, au_fname, phone, contract)
        VALUES ('453-12-3255', 'Smith', 'John', '400 486-234', 1)

DELETE FROM authors WHERE au_id = '672-71-3249'
```

2. Manually start the replication process.

3. Check to see if the rows changed in the subscription database. For example:

```
SELECT * FROM authors
```

Resulting Context

This implementation has all benefits and liabilities of the *Snapshot Replication* pattern. This section describes additional benefits and liabilities.

Benefits

- **Compressed snapshots.** SQL Server gives you the option of compressing the snapshot file. This option is useful when you have to transmit the snapshot over a slow communications link, or when the snapshot file will not fit on removable media. Using compressed snapshots saves disk space, which decreases transmission time and network load.

- **Integrated into SQL Server Enterpise Manager.** The configuration and execution of a replication in SQL Server is integrated into the SQL Server administration and can be easily done with SQL Server Enterprise Manager.

Liabilities

- **Disk space requirements for snapshots.** Because SQL Server stores the snapshot file in a separate folder and the file grows with the volume of the replication set, you must provide an appropriate amount of free disk space.

- **Overhead of compressing snapshots.** The disadvantage of compressing snapshots is that this option increases the time required to generate and apply snapshots.

- **Additional database to be managed.** The implementation requires the distribution database as an additional database that must be managed.

Hint: This pattern is appropriate for replication sets that change infrequently, or for those with a substantial amount of changed data. It is also often used to distribute read-only copies of data as it appears at a specific moment in time (for example, for analytical purposes such as decision support).

This pattern is also frequently used to populate a database for the first time. In cases where you must transmit a large volume of data to the target, you can use removable media instead of a communications link.

Testing Considerations

After you set up the replication link as described in pattern, you must test it thoroughly. Your test cases should cover the following scenarios at a minimum:

- Correct transmission of the snapshot that includes the replication set
- Network interruption between the distribution database and the subscription database during a running transmission
- A hard abort of the subscription database during a running transmission

After each test, make sure that the subscription database is in the correct state.

Security Considerations

To secure the connection between the Distributor and the Subscribers, do one of the following:

- Use a SQL Server user account to connect to the Distributor.
- Place all computers in one Windows domain, or have a common user with the same password on all computers. Then use a trusted Windows connection between Distributor and Subscribers.

Note: The SQL Server Agents on all systems must run on a local or a domain account, not on the local system account. Otherwise, the replication will not work.

Snapshot data can reside in places other than the source and target data. Use the same security standards for snapshot data that you use for other data in the replication.

Operational Considerations

The SQL Server Agent manages the different jobs of the replication. Schedules for these jobs are defined during the configuration. Alternatively, you can start each job manually using the SQL Server Enterprise Manager.

The Replication Monitor in SQL Server Enterprise Manager provides the following information:

- A list of all publications and attached agents with the time and the duration of the last execution and information about the last action
- A list of all agents grouped by task with current status and a history of actions
- The event log entries created by Replication Alerts, which monitor the replication process

If the replication fails, do the following:

- Check to see if the accounts have network access rights.
- Check the history of the subscription to determine the reason the synchronization failed.
- Check the Replication Monitor for highlighted replication failures.

The connections between the Publisher and its Subscribers must be able to manage the load. If the Publisher sends its data to Subscribers over a slow or expensive communications link, using the republisher model will improve replication. In any case, the Publisher must be connected to remote Distributors by reliable, high-speed communications links.

Hint: An alternative for the transmission of the replication set to use removable media to transmit the snapshot from source to target.

Related Patterns

For more information, see the following related patterns.

Patterns that May Have Led You Here

- *Move Copy of Data*. This pattern is the root pattern of this cluster; it presents the overall architecture for maintaining copies of data.

- *Data Replication*. This pattern presents the architecture of data replication, which is a particular way of moving copies of data.

- *Master-Slave Replication*. This pattern describes design considerations for transmitting data from the source to the target by overwriting potential changes in the target on a higher level than the *Master-Slave Snapshot Replication*.

- *Master-Slave Snapshot Replication*. This pattern presents a solution that transmits the whole replication set from the source to the target on each transmission.

Other Patterns of Interest

- *Implementing Master-Slave Transactional Incremental Replication Using SQL Server*. This pattern uses a snapshot replication to prepare the target.

- *Implementing Master-Master Row-Level Synchronization Using SQL Server*. This pattern uses a snapshot replication to prepare the target.

Implementing Master-Slave Transactional Incremental Replication Using SQL Server

Context

You want to build a *Master-Slave Transactional Incremental Replication* between two Microsoft® SQL Server™ databases, and you want to take advantage of the integrated replication functionality of SQL Server.

The schemas of the source and target do not need to be identical; simple manipulations as defined in the *Data Replication* pattern can be implemented in the replication link. In addition, horizontal (row) and vertical (column) filters can be used to restrict the replication set.

Note: This pattern uses terms and concepts from the following data patterns:
- *Move Copy of Data*
- *Data Replication*
- *Master-Slave Transactional Incremental Replication*

Background

Before introducing the implementation with SQL Server, this pattern covers the following topics:

- A summary of the replication building block, as described in the *Master-Slave Transactional Incremental Replication* pattern
- The SQL Server replication services that this pattern uses (SQL Server transactional replication).
- The mapping of the elements of the replication building block to the services of SQL Server

Replication Building Block

The *replication building block* used in the *Master-Slave Transactional Incremental Replication* pattern consists of a source and a target that are connected by a replication link, as Figure 3.43 (on the next page) shows.

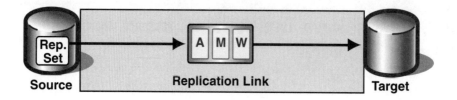

A = Acquire
M = Manipulate
W = Write
Rep. Set = Replication Set
Figure 3.43
Replication building block

Source

The source contains the replication set, which is the data copied from the source and sent across a data movement link to the target.

Acquire

The Acquire service reads the data changes that are replicated.

Manipulate

The Manipulate service performs simple data transformations, such as data type conversions and splitting or combining columns.

Write

The Write service updates the target with the manipulated rows.

Target

The target is the database where the replication set is to be written.

The process of moving the replication set from source to target according to defined functional and operational requirements is called a transmission.

SQL Server Transactional Replication

SQL Server replication uses several standard services to move data from a publication database to a subscription database. Figure 3.44 shows the services and processes involved in SQL Server transactional replication.

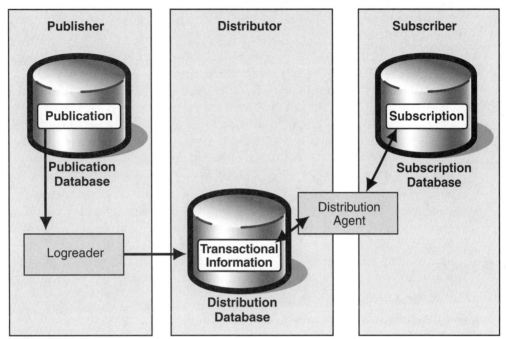

Figure 3.44
SQL Server transactional replication

Platform Roles

SQL Server defines three roles for the platforms involved in the replication:

- **Publisher.** The Publisher contains the source and the Log Reader Agent. In this environment, the Subscriber defines the replication set (publication) to be replicated.

- **Distributor.** The Distributor holds the distribution database. It runs the cleanup jobs for managing the distribution database, and in a push replication also runs the Distribution Agent.

- **Subscriber.** The Subscriber contains the target and creates a subscription to subscribe a publication. In a pull replication, the Subscriber runs the Distribution Agent.

The Distributor does not necessarily need to be a separate platform. Its role can also be assigned to the Publisher, where it is called a local Distributor. Otherwise, it is called a remote Distributor.

Software Components

SQL Server transactional replication consists of two main processes and a database:

- **Log Reader Agent.** The Log Reader Agent extracts changes defined by the publication from the transaction log of the publication database, and stores the changes to be replicated in an additional database, called the distribution database.

- **Distribution database.** The distribution database is a SQL Server database and is located on the Publisher (called a local Distributor), or on a dedicated platform (called a remote Distributor). Because it stores changes in a proprietary format, the distribution database can only be used for SQL Server replication, not for any applications. After the Log Reader Agent extracts the changes, the logging system of the publication database is allowed to shrink the transaction log, because the information for the transmissions is saved in the distribution database.

- **Distribution Agent.** The Distribution Agent applies the initial snapshot to the subscription database by moving transactions held in the distribution database to Subscribers. The Distribution Agent runs at either the distributor for push subscriptions, or at the Subscriber for pull subscriptions. Before actually writing the changes, the Distribution Agent can manipulate them using a Data Transmission Services (DTS) package that the Subscriber defines. If you need to perform manipulations before writing the changes to the subscription database, you can do so using such a DTS package.

Independent of the replication processes, **cleanup jobs** run on the distribution database and perform the following tasks:

- **Agent History Clean Up: Distribution.** Removes replication agent history from the distribution database.

- **Distribution Clean Up: Distribution.** Removes replicated transactions from the distribution database.

- **Expired Subscription Clean Up.** Detects and removes expired subscriptions from publication databases.

- **Reinitialize Subscriptions Having Data Validation Failures.** Reinitializes all subscriptions that have data validation failures.

- **Replication Agents Checkup.** Detects replication agents that are not actively logging history.

A SQL Server replication is based on the following rules:

- Any table that should be published needs a primary key as a unique identifier for a row.

- SQL Server transactional replication assumes that the subscription database is read-only (unless updating subscriptions are used). This means:

    - Any changes to the subscription database at the Subscriber will be overwritten by the next transmission.

    - Any deletion of rows on the subscription database will cause a failure in the replication process.

Mapping the Replication Building Block to SQL Server

SQL Server transactional replication implements the replication building block elements used by *Master-Slave Transactional Incremental Replication* as shown in Figure 3.45. Figure 3.45 is the result of merging Figures 3.43 and 3.44.

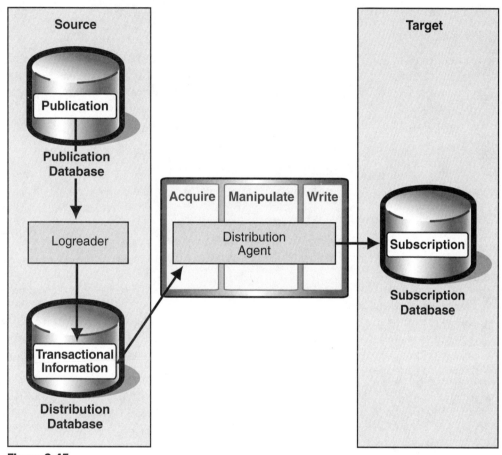

Figure 3.45
SQL Server implementation of Master-Slave Transactional Incremental Replication

Source

Incremental replication transmits only the changes that have been made to source rows that the target has copies of, rather than getting full refreshes of the data. As described in the design pattern *Master-Slave Transactional Incremental Replication*, this type of replication needs a recording of the source transactions to use for change transmission. SQL Server replication preserves the changes to the publication database in the distribution database for transmission to the subscription database. The distribution database is updated by the Log Reader Agent, which reads the transactional information from the transaction log of the relational database management system (RDBMS) and writes it to the distribution database. This allows the RDBMS to shrink the transaction log.

The changes remain available in the distribution database for a specified period of time (the retention period).

Replication Set

In SQL Server, the replication set to be replicated from the publication database to the subscription database is called a publication. A publication consists of one or more tables, or only parts of tables. You can define the parts of tables in one of two ways:

- Filter the rows to be replicated by defining a search condition.

  In the theory of relational databases, the result is called a *restriction*.

- Filter the columns to be replicated as a subset of the table's columns.

  In the theory of relational databases, the result is called a *projection*.

Acquire

The Distribution Agent reads all the changed data from the distribution database from the last transmission up to the most recent transaction.

Manipulate

The Distribution Agent can manipulate the data. When the Subscriber registers its subscription to the Distributor, it can define a DTS package, which the Distribution Agent invokes before sending the data to the Subscriber. Each Subscriber can use its own package, so different Subscribers can get various views of the same data.

Within such a DTS package, you can define any manipulations that can be performed using the data of the current row and the ActiveX script language. Each row from the publication database can result in only one row at the subscription database, or it can be skipped. Columns can be split or combined. Additionally, any kind of data type conversions and changes of column names can be done.

Write

The Distribution Agent writes the data to the subscription database. The Write is done by default using a stored procedure. Optionally, it can be done directly using SQL.

In general, the Distribution Agent writes the changes regardless of whether the contents of the subscription database have been updated by any application. If you must prevent updates from being overwritten, you have to use updateable subscribers or configure a merge replication instead of a transactional replication. A merge replication is described in the pattern *Implementing Master-Master Row-Level Synchronization Using SQL Server*.

Target

The target is the subscription database, which contains the replication set to be updated.

Implementation Strategy

To set up a new replication link, follow these steps:

1. Configure the Distributor:

    a. Create the distribution database: This is an internal SQL Server database used from the Distributor. In most cases, you use the default options to create this database, but you can also customize it.

    b. Choose the snapshot folder: You can either choose the default folder for exchanging the initial snapshot files or use a custom folder.

    c. Set up the Subscriber parameter: To define the default parameter for all subscribers, you can confirm the offered configuration options or customize them.

2. Define the publication:

    a. Select the publication database that includes the publication.

    b. Decide if you want to transform the data during the transmission. If so, any subscriber must have a DTS package for the transformation.

    c. Select the possible database systems the Subscribers will use: SQL Server 2000, earlier versions of SQL Server, or another RDBMS.

    d. For each table, specify whether the entire table should be replicated, or restrict the table by specifying horizontal and vertical filters.

    e. Decide whether anonymous Subscribers are allowed to subscribe to the publication.

    f. Decide how often the Snapshot Agent creates a new snapshot.

3. Create a DTS package for the transformation, if you have decided to use one.

4. Define the subscription:

    a. Decide if you want a pull or a push subscription.

    b. Select the publication you want to subscribe to.

    c. Choose the subscription database.

    d. Decide if you want to initialize the subscriber using an initial snapshot from the publisher.

    e. If you want to start the transmission automatically, define a schedule.

    f. Specify the DTS package you want to use for this subscriber.

    g. Verify that all required services are started.

At this point, all parts of the replication link have been configured. From now on, both Publisher and Subscriber will log all changes to the specified replication set using triggers.

The SQL Server transactional replication runs different jobs:

- Snapshot Agent: Creates the initial snapshot on the Publisher.
- Distribution Agent: Applies the snapshots on the Subscriber.
- Cleanup jobs: Clean up the distribution database on the Distributor.

The example that follows describes in detail how to use the SQL Server wizards to set up such a replication link.

Example

This example shows how to configure transactional replication based on a particular replication set. The replication set used here is the authors table from the pubs sample database, which is delivered with SQL Server.

Overview

The environment has two SQL Server computers: PUB_SERVER and SUBS_SERVER. The Publisher has a database, PUB_DB, that contains the authors table from the pubs sample database. To use PUB_SERVER as a local Distributor, you create a distribution database named Distribution. The Subscriber has an empty database, SUBS_DB. Figure 3.46 shows the environment of the example.

This configuration creates a periodical incremental transactional replication process with an initial snapshot. The Subscriber initiates the replication (pull) every 15 minutes. The data from the Publisher is manipulated during the replication by converting the first and the last name from the authors table into uppercase. (This example does not allow updateable or anonymous subscribers.)

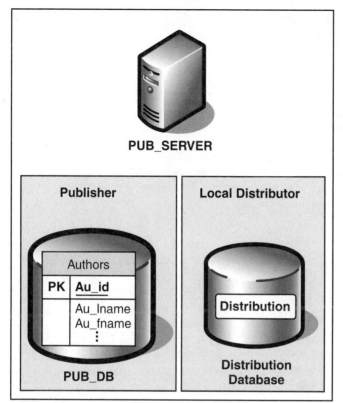 

Figure 3.46
Example environment

Configuring the Publisher and the Distributor

To set up the example environment, follow these steps in the Configure Publishing and Distribution Wizard:

1. In SQL Server Enterprise Manager, select the publication database server, right-click **Replication**, and then click **Configure Publishing, Subscribers and Distribution**.

2. On the **Select Distributor** page, select the **Make *Pub_Server* its own Distributor** option, where *Pub_Server* is the name of the server you want to configure as a distributor. Click **Next**.

Note: The Distributor can be located on the same server as the Publisher, in which case it is called a local Distributor, or on a remote server. This example uses a local Distributor.

---

3. On the **Specify Snapshot Folder** page, type the name of a shared folder on the Publisher where the Snapshot Agent can store snapshot files.

> **Note:** You must create and share this folder manually, or use a previously defined system shared folder for this purpose.

4. On the **Customize the Configuration** page, select **No, use the following default settings** to create a default distribution database.

> **Note:** In this simple example, it is sufficient to use the default settings. In a more complex environment, you should manually configure the distribution database.

Creating a Publication

Next, use the Create Publication Wizard to create a publication on the Publisher.

1. In SQL Server Enterprise Manager, select the publication database server, expand **Replication,** right-click **Publications**, and then click **New Publication**.

2. On the **Welcome Screen,** check the **Show advanced options** check box to use this wizard with the advanced options needed to enable a transformation of the data.

3. On the **Choose Publication Database** page, select *Pub_DB* as the publication database, where *Pub_DB* is the name of your database for the replication.

4. On the **Select Publication Type** page, select **Transactional Publication** to create a publication for a transactional replication.

5. You do not want to allow the replication of changes from the subscriber to the publisher; therefore, ensure that no option is selected on the **Updateable Subscription** page.

6. On the **Transform Published Data** page, select **Yes, transform the data** to enable the transformation during the replication.

7. On the **Specify Subscriber Types** page, select only **Servers running SQL Server 2000**.

8. The **Specify Articles** page shows possible objects for replication in the publication database. From the **Object Type Tables** list, select the table **authors**.

> **Note:** Clicking the ellipses (**...**) button for each object shows additional properties for the replication. You do not need them in this example.

9. On the **Select Publication Name and Description** page, specify the **Publication name** as **example**. The default publication description can be used.

10. On the **Customize the Properties of the Publication** page, select the option beginning with **No, create the publication as specified**, because you can use the defaults options shown in the text box below the options.

11. On the **Completing the Create Publication Wizard** page, click **Finish** to create the publication.

Defining a DTS Package for the Transformation

Before you can create a subscription for the defined publication, you must create a DTS package for the transformation.

1. In SQL Server Enterprise Manager, select the publication database server, expand **Replication,** open **Publications,** right-click on the **example:pub_db** replication, and then click **Properties**.

2. On the **Publication Properties** page, click the**Subscriptions** tab and then click **Transformations**.

3. On the **Welcome Screen,** click **Next**.

4. On the **Choose a Destination** page, select the subscription database server and database. (See Figure 3.47.)

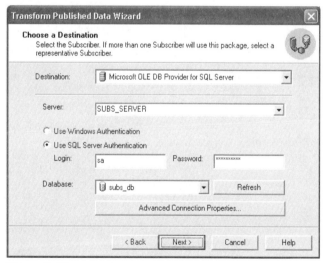

Figure 3.47
Choose a Destination page

5. On the **Define Transformations** page, click the ellipses (...) button from the article authors.

6. On the **Column Mappings** tab of the **Column Mappings and Transformations** page, select **Drop the existing table and recreate it** from the list box. Leave the mappings unchanged. (See Figure 3.48 on the next page.)

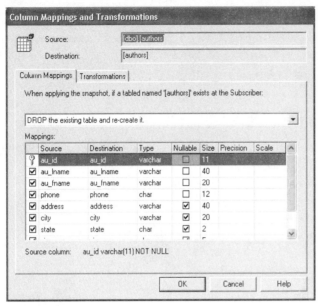

Figure 3.48
Column Mappings tab on the Column Mappings and Transformations page

7. Click the Transformations tab. Click Transform data using the following script and select VB Script Language from the list box. (See Figure 3.49.)

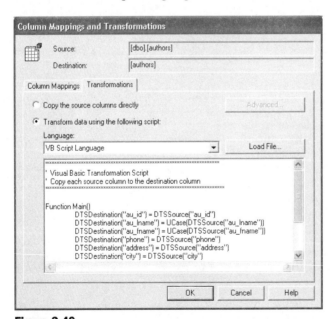

Figure 3.49
Transformations tab on the Column Mappings and Transformations page

8. Use the following code to transform the first and the last name of the author to uppercase:

```
Function Main()
    DTSDestination("au_id") = DTSSource("au_id")
    DTSDestination("au_lname") = UCase(DTSSource("au_lname"))
    DTSDestination("au_fname") = UCase(DTSSource("au_fname"))
    DTSDestination("phone") = DTSSource("phone")
    DTSDestination("address") = DTSSource("address")
    DTSDestination("city") = DTSSource("city")
    DTSDestination("state") = DTSSource("state")
    DTSDestination("zip") = DTSSource("zip")
    DTSDestination("contract") = DTSSource("contract")
    Main = DTSTransformStat_OK
End Function
```

9. On the **DTS Package Location** page, select the option to save the package on the Distributor. Use the SQL Server authentication option, and insert the user and the password to connect to the Distributor.

10. On the **DTS Package Identification** page, specify the name of the package. In this example, the name should be **transform_sub**. You do not need to define an owner password.

11. On the **Completing the Transform Published Data Wizard** page, click **Finish** to save the package as specified.

Creating a Subscription

To complete the configuration you must create a pull subscription for the defined publication on the Subscriber.

1. In SQL Server Enterprise Manager, select the subscription database server, expand **Replication,** right-click **Subscriptions**, and then click **New Pull Subscription**.

2. On the **Welcome Screen,** click **Next**.

3. On the **Look for Publications** page, select **Look at publications from registered servers**.

4. On the **Choose Publication** page, expand **PUB_SERVER** and select the publication named **example:pub_db**, where *PUB_SERVER* is the name of your Publisher and *example:pub_db* is the name of your publication. (See Figure 3.50 on the next page.)

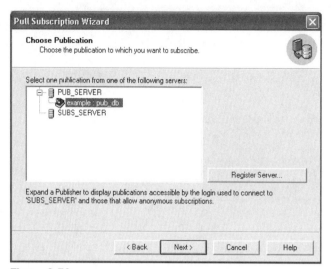

Figure 3.50
Choose Publication page

5. On the **Specify Synchronization Agent Login** page, select **Use SQL Server Authentication**. Enter the login and the password of a user account that is used to connect to the Publisher during the replication.

6. On the **Choose Destination Database** page, select **Subs_DB** as the database for the subscription, where *Subs_DB* is the name of your subscription database.

7. On the **Initialize Subscription** page, select **Yes, initialize the schema and the data**.

8. On the **Snapshot Delivery** page, specify the snapshot folder. Use the default folder of the publication.

9. On the **Set Distribution Agent Schedule** page, select **Using the following schedule** and click **Change** to specify a new schedule for the Distribution Agent.

10. On the **Edit Recurring Job Schedule** page, define the schedule for the Distribution Agent as a daily run with an interval of 15 minutes. (See Figure 3.51.)

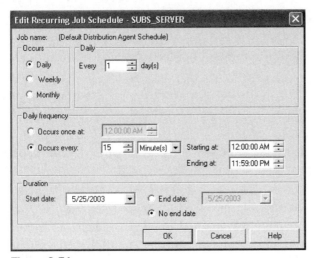

Figure 3.51
Edit Recurring Job Schedule page

11. On the **Specify DTS Package** page, select **Distributor** and click **List packages**. For the transformation, select the **transform_sub** package that you created previously. (See Figure 3.52.)

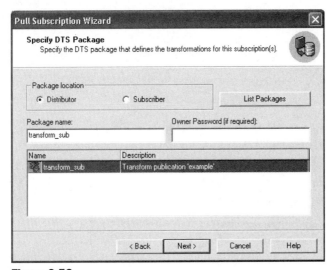

Figure 3.52
Specify DTS Package page

12. The **Start Required Services** page shows the status of the SQL Server Agent on the Subscriber. If the SQL Server Agent is not running, select the check box next to the entry for the agent. The agent will be started after the wizard creates the subscription.

13. On the **Completing the Pull Subscription Wizard** page, review the options for the specified subscription. Click **Finish** to create the subscription with these options.

The configuration process is finished. Before starting the first transmission, the following checks should be done:

- Did the Snapshot Agent create the first initial snapshot? It may be necessary to start the Snapshot Agent manually on the publication database.

- Did the Pull Agent initialize the schema and the first replication? If this has not been done automatically, you can start the process manually on the subscription database.

Starting and Restarting the Synchronization

1. In the Enterprise Manager, select the publication database server, expand **Replication Monitor,** select **Publishers**, **Pub_Server**, and open the publication **example:pub_db**.

2. Right-click the **Snapshot Agent** and select **Start Agent** to create an initial snapshot.

3. Right-click **SUBS_Server:subs_db** and select **Start Synchronizing** to start the transactional replication.

Testing the Example

You can easily test the functionality of the implemented replication by changing some data in the publication, starting the replication process, and checking to see if the Subscriber has changed accordingly.

To check various kinds of data changes, perform INSERT, UPDATE, and DELETE operations on the data in the publication database.

1. Change data in the publication database. For example:

```
UPDATE authors SET au_lname = 'Smith' WHERE au_id = '807-91-6654'

INSERT INTO authors (au_id, au_lname, au_fname, phone, contract)
        VALUES ('453-12-3255', 'Smith', 'John', '400 486-234', 1)

DELETE FROM authors WHERE au_id = '672-71-3249'
```

2. Manually start the replication process.

3. Check to see if the rows changed in the subscription database. For example:

```
SELECT * FROM authors
```

Resulting Context

Although this pattern describes a replication between SQL Server databases, the subscription database can be any heterogeneous database that provides an ODBC or OLEDB interface, such as Oracle, DB2, or Microsoft Access.

Note: To use a heterogeneous database as a publication database, you need a software component that implements a dedicated interface — the replication distributor interface. The examples that are delivered with SQL Server show how to implement this software.

There are two ways to use a heterogeneous database as a subscription databse:

- Use ODBC or OLEDB and create a push subscription using the wizard on the Publisher. This is the simplest way to publish data to a heterogeneous Subscriber.
- Create a publication and then create an application with an embedded distribution control. The embedded control implements the pull subscription from the Subscriber to the Publisher.

For Subscribers, the subscribing database has no administrative capabilities regarding the replication being performed.

A closer look at the architecture of the SQL Server elements reveals that the implementation corresponds to a cascading synchronization with two replication links. One link is from the publication database to the distribution database, and the other link is from the distribution database to the subscription database. The distribution database plays the role of a cascade intermediary target/source (CITS). It can serve additional replications links to other targets. The *Master-Slave Cascading Replication* pattern descibes this design and the terms associated with it.

This pattern inherits the benefits and liabilities from the pattern *Master-Slave Transactional Incremental Replication*. Because this pattern actually implements a cascading replication, it also inherits the benefits and liabilities of the *Master-Slave Cascading Replication* pattern. The use of this pattern also results in the following additional benefits and liabilities:

Benefits

- **Integrated logging mechanism.** If you track the transaction log, you do not need a logging mechanism for changes in the application or database.
- **Integrated into SQL Server Enterpise Manager.** The configuration and execution of the replication in SQL Server is integrated in the SQL Server administration, and can be easily done with the SQL Server Enterprise Manager.

Liabilities

- **Additional database to be managed.** The implementation requires the distribution database as an additional database that must be managed.

Testing Considerations

After you set up the replication link as described in this pattern, you must test it thoroughly. Your test cases should cover these scenarios and others:

- Correct transmission of transactions that update the replication set
- The largest transaction that might occur
- The longest disconnection between Publisher and Subscriber that you expect under production conditions
- Network interruption between the Publisher and the distribution database during transactions on the Publisher, if you are using a remote distributor. (This does not apply to the example in this pattern.)
- Network interruption between the distribution database and the Subscriber during a a running transmission
- A hard abort of the database system on the Subscriber during a running transmission

After each test, make sure that the Subscription is in the correct state.

Also make sure that transactions that do not update the replication set are not transmitted.

Finally, put the highest expected load on the Publisher and verify that the replication still runs correctly.

Security Considerations

To secure the connection between the Distributor and the Subscribers, do one of the following:

- Use a SQL Server user account to connect to the Distributor.
- Place all computers in one Microsoft Windows® domain, or have a common user with the same password on all computers. Then use a trusted Windows connection between Distributor and Subscribers.

If you prefer a security approach that is independent of the operating system, you should use SQL Server authentication.

Note: The SQL Server Agents on all systems must run on a local or a domain account, not on the local system account. Otherwise, the replication does not work.

Operational Considerations

The SQL Server Agent manages the different jobs of the replication. Schedules for these jobs are defined during the configuration. Alternatively, you can start each job using the SQL Server Enterprise Manager.

The Replication Monitor in SQL Server Enterprise Manager provides the following information:

- A list of all publications and attached agents with the time and the duration of the last execution and information about the last action
- A list of all agents grouped by task with current status and a history of actions
- The event log entries created by Replication Alerts, which watch the replication process.

If a row was deleted on the subscription database and the transmission tries to change this row, an error occurs. In this case, there are two solutions:

- Manually restore the row in the subscription database by using an INSERT statement based on the data from the same row in the publication database.
- Have the replication automatically use a new snapshot to rebuild the subscription database. This snaphot must be newer than the first erroneous transmission.

If the replication fails, do the following:

- Check to see if the accounts have network access rights.
- Check the history of the subscription to determine the reason the synchronization failed.
- Check the Replication Monitor for highlighted replication failures.

The replication usually runs on a defined schedule. If you want to test the replication or start the merge replication immediately, however, you need to start the replication manually.

Hints: It is common practice to have the distribution database on the same server as the Publisher, for example to ensure frequent and rapid movement of the transactional information from the transaction log to the distribution database.

If there are many subscribers and a high rate of operations on the publisher, the Distributor can become a bottleneck. In this case, you should configure the Distributor on an additional server to separate the transmissions from the activity caused by the applications.

Transferring a large amount of data over slow conections can be problematic. An alternate solution is to create the initial snapshot files and transaction data using removeable media, replicate the database, and then establish the transactional replication over the slow network.

Related Patterns

For more information, see the following related patterns:

Patterns that May Have Led You Here

- *Move Copy of Data.* This pattern is the root pattern of this cluster; it presents the overall architecture for maintaining copies of data.
- *Data Replication.* This pattern presents the architecture of data replication, which is a particular way of moving copies of data.
- *Master-Slave Replication.* This pattern describes design considerations for transmitting data from the source to the target by overwriting potential changes in the target on a higher level than the *Master-Slave Snapshot Replication.*
- *Master-Slave Transactional Incremental Replication.* This pattern presents a solution that transmits only the changes from the source to the target on a transaction-by-transaction basis.

Other Patterns of Interest

- *Master-Slave Snapshot Replication.* This pattern presents the design of snapshot replications, which this pattern uses to prepare the target.

Master-Slave Cascading Replication

Context

You are designing a replication solution for the following requirements:

- A replication set is to be replicated from a single source to many targets that all require substantially the same replication data.

- The replicated data in the targets is read-only, or if it is updated at the targets by any applications, it is accepted that these updates can be overwritten by later transmissions. This is called a master-slave relationship.

Hence the replication flow is one-way, from the source to the targets, and neither conflict detection nor conflict resolution are triggered at the targets because of target changes.

Figure 3.53 summarizes this overall replication scenario.

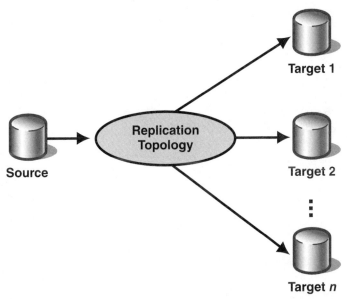

Figure 3.53
Overall replication scenario

You know you could design direct replication links from the source to each target, but the potential impact on the source, and possibly the source availability, is a concern. Therefore, you want to find another approach that reduces this concern and is also an efficient way to replicate this common replication set to many targets.

Problem

How can you optimize the replication to a set of targets in a master-slave environment, and minimize the impact on the source?

Forces

Any of the following **compelling forces** would justify using the solution described in this pattern:

- **Too many passes on the source.** Every replication link that starts from a source requires a pass over the replication set to acquire it. The resources (for example, CPU time and I/O activity) needed for the required number of passes might not be available on the source database server, or they may cost too much.

- **Very large replication set.** Even with a moderate number of replication links to the source, the total overhead on the source database server can become unsustainable if the amount of data to be transmitted to the targets is large.

- **Significant growth in replication needs anticipated.** Concerning both of the preceding forces, you anticipate a significant growth in the number of targets and amount of data to be transmitted. Therefore it is important to implement a replication topology that can sustain the predicted growth.

- **Need to offload replication set from source as quickly as possible.** Acquiring data impacts source resources and you must minimize the duration of the impact. For example, if you are replicating across a slow communications link, you may prefer to offload the source quickly and then replicate to the target from this offloaded set.

- **No direct connection between source and target.** Due to your network topology, you might not be able to directly link the source and target, but you can connect to a third place.

The following **enabling forces** facilitate the move to the solution, and their absence could hinder such a move:

- **Targets can tolerate the delays implied by replication.** The timeliness with which the data arrives at any one of the targets depends on the replication link, which frequently includes a network link. Adding more replication links from the source to the final target generally increases the delay until changes made to the source replication set appear at the target.

- **Great similarity in the replication sets to be replicated.** The core of this pattern is that all the replication data comes from the same original source replication set. Within this fundamental constraint, each replication link can have its own replication set to be replicated, which can differ from the replication set of other replication links. Although the structure differences between each source/target pair might be fairly small, the overall differences could be significant. *Data Replication* requires that the source and the target of every replication building block be very similar. *Master-Slave Cascading Replication* requires the similarity of all databases along the whole chain of replication links to be high. Otherwise, an *Extract-Transform-Load (ETL)* approach would be more useful.

Solution

Increase the number of replication links between the source and target by adding one or more intermediary targets between the original source and the end target databases, as Figure 3.53 shows. Specifically, this arrangement adds the concept of *cascade intermediary target/source (CITS)* to the topology, as Figure 3.54 shows. These intermediaries are data stores that take a replication set from the source, and thus act as a target in a first replication link. Then they act as sources to move the data to the next replication link and so on until they reach the *cascade end targets (CETs)*.

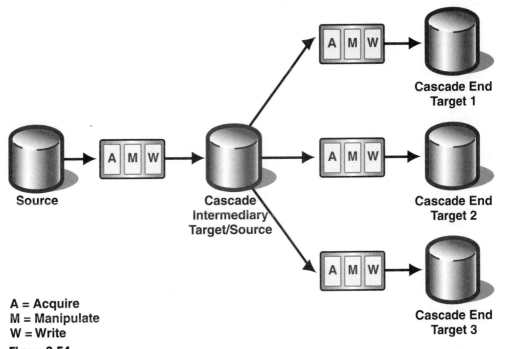

A = Acquire
M = Manipulate
W = Write

Figure 3.54
Master-Slave Cascading Replication with a single intermediate target/source

Figure 3.54 shows a very simple example of a *Master-Slave Cascading Replication* topology. Each Acquire, Manipulate, and Write (AMW) box in the figure represents a replication link. For more information about the replication building block, see the *Data Replication* pattern.

In general, several CITSs can be connected to the same source and a CITS can also be connected to several other CITSs. Regardless of the number of CITS, *Master-Slave*

Cascading Replication arranges them in a tree with the source as the root, CITS as inner nodes, and CETs as the leaf nodes.

For discussion purposes, it is helpful to define a few more specific terms for the replication links in a topology:

- **Initial link.** The *initial link* connects a source to a CITS.
- **Intermediary link.** The *intermediary link* connects a CITS to another CITS.
- **End link.** The *end link* connects a CITS to a CET.

The characteristics of the end links are the same as if the targets were connected to the source directly. This means that the end links can be configured for full or incremental replication depending on the requirements, and that they can start a transmission immediately after every transaction, periodically, or on demand.

Hint: The addition of CITS to the replication topology, however, impacts the service level offered to the CETs. The initial and intermediary links must transmit any data or changes early enough for any of the following intermediary or end links. Thus, it is common practice to design an immediate replication here. If all end links only do periodic or on-demand replication, a periodic replication on the initial and intermediary links would be sufficient. For these reasons, you should not design an on-demand replication on an initial or intermediary link, because the timeliness of some of the CITS and their corresponding targets would depend on a user or operator starting the transmission.

The choice of the replication frequency also impacts the choice of the replication refresh policy. If the initial and intermediary links have been configured for immediate replication, you will have to use incremental replication to transmit only the changes. Incremental replication is also generally the best choice to transmit changes for periodic replication at the initial and intermediary links. If the replication sets are small enough, another option is to use a snapshot replication on the initial and intermediary replication links.

Next Considerations

To design a *Master-Slave Cascading Replication* topology for your environment, you must do the following:

- Determine the number of CITS to use.
- Design the replication links from the source to the CITS and from the CITS to the CETs.
- Determine how much data is required for each CITS.
- Define the data structure of the CITSs.
- Define the manipulation in each replication link.

The following sections explore these issues.

Number of CITSs

A single CITS removes most of the load from the source database server because there is only a single replication link from the source to the CITS. Thus, the only overhead to the source is that single replication link.

However, if you design just a single CITS, you introduce two new single points of failure: the CITS and the additional replication link. An additional CITS helps to mitigate this effect because you can design an alternative chain of replication links from the source to each of the targets. Although the additional replication links that are now connected to the source cause a slight increase in replication overhead compared to a single replication link, the overall availability increases because the alternative chain acts as a backup to the standard chain.

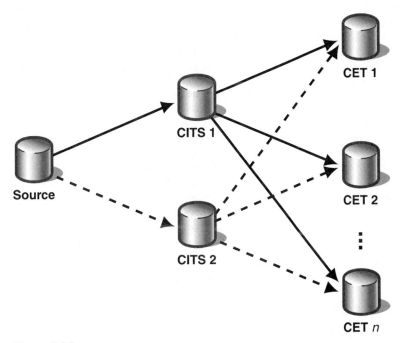

Figure 3.55
Master-Slave Cascading Replication with an alternative chain (dotted arrows)

Hint: After you have two (or more) CITSs connected to the source, you can connect parts of the CETs to each of them. This achieves some load balancing on the CITSs because every CITS serves fewer CETs. In case of a failure, the CETs are served by one of the remaining CITSs.

The replication links to both CITSs must transmit the same replication set. Additionally, the CITSs must not be written to by any process but the replication link from the source. If one of these conditions fails, the CITSs could have different data. In that case, they would not be able to serve as substitutes for each other.

More CITSs can also be added if a single CITS cannot serve all CETs. Adding CITSs also increases scalability because you can add new CITSs to accommodate a growing number of CETs. If the number of CITSs consequently impacts the source in an unsustainable way, you can even add another layer of CITSs. This increases the chain length by one replication link, but again frees the source database server from the additional load.

Hint: Adding CITSs can also help you optimize for different replication characteristics because the CITSs can be structured in different ways. If, for example, some of the CETs require snapshot replication, while others require incremental replication, you can optimize the structure of one of the CITS for storing change data and the other one for storing the data itself. The CETs requesting the changes will connect to the first CITS, while the CETs requesting snapshots will connect to CETs that are optimized for the snapshots. Generally, you should look for clusters of CETs with similar replication characteristics and then design a dedicated CITS for each of these clusters. Thereafter, you can optimize every CITS to best support the replications links that have similar characteristics.

Limiting the Number of Replication Links

You must have at least one chain of replication links between the source and every CET to transmit the data or its changes. As described earlier, you can design an alternative chain of replication links from the source to every target to achieve higher availability for the whole system. Do not overdo it by designing too many alternative chains, however, because the additional replication links increase the load on the source. It is best to design at most one standard chain of replication links plus one alternative chain. Furthermore, designing additional replication links should be reserved for when you feel that normal data availability techniques, such as clustering, storage area networks, or hot standbys, are not suitable.

Amount of Data for Each CITS

The source replication set which is stored on each CITS must satisfy the requirements of all the CETs connected. Thus, the amount of data stored on each CITS is the logical union of data requested by any of its CETs and the type of replication being used.

Data Structure for Each CITS

To determine the data structure for each CITS involves, choose one of the following design options:

- **Matching the data structure of the CITS to the source.** This enables the movement of data from the source to the CITS without any additional manipulation overhead. This design is important if the main goal of your cascading replication is to remove any avoidable load from the source.

- **Matching the data structure of the CITS to the CET superset.** In this case, the manipulation is performed only once, namely within the replication link from the source to the CITS. The targets can be fed easily by the contents of the CITS. This provides a higher overall efficiency with the tradeoff of some impact on the source that could have been avoided.

- **Designing a data structure that differs from both the source and the CETs.** If all replication links to the CETs perform incremental replication, the CITSs do not have to store the data—only the changes. In this case, the data structure of the CITSs can be designed for the storage of changes only.

Examples

The following examples present two possible configurations of *Master-Slave Cascading Replication*.

Different Lengths of Replication Chains

This first example assumes that you have a single source and a large number of CETs. A small number of the CETs receive snapshots, while the others are served by incremental replication. The snapshot replication is transmitted by way of a single CITS. The number of CETs served by incremental replication is too large to be served by a single CITS, however. To minimize the impact on the source, you could design two levels of CITS, each with a single CITS that is connected to the source. Figure 3.56 on the next page shows the resulting replication topology where thick arrows represent replication links with snapshot replication and thin arrows represent replication links with incremental replication.

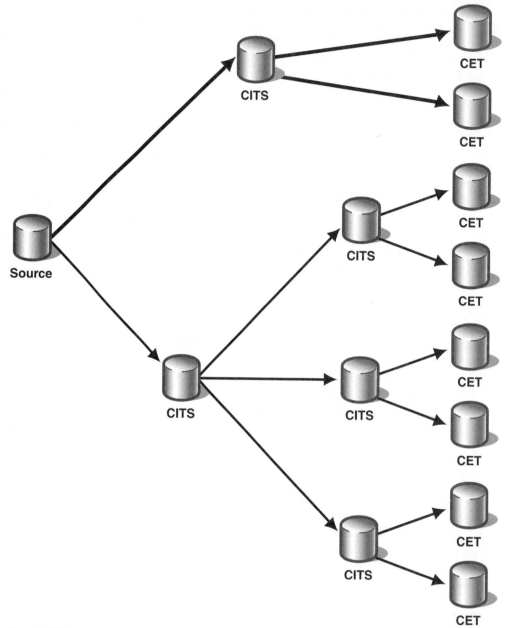

Figure 3.56
Master-Slave Cascading Replication topology with different chain lengths

Two Sources and Conflict Detection and Resolution

Figure 3.57 shows a replication topology in which a CET participates in two master-slave cascading replications.

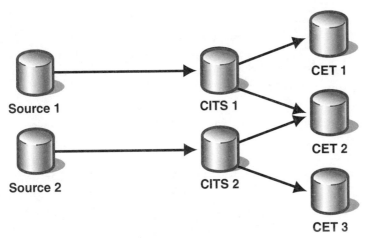

Figure 3.57
Master-Slave Cascading Replication from two sources

If the replication sets of Source 1 and Source 2 do not intersect, then replication from Source 1 by way of CITS 1 to CET 2 always affects different records than those from Source 2 by way of CITS 2. Thus, no special attention is required in CET 2 to handle both replication chains.

However, if the replication sets of Source 1 and Source 2 do intersect, the same CET 2 record can be affected by both the replication from Source 1 through CITS 1 and Source 2 through CITS 2. Resolving the discrepancy requires the ability to detect and resolve conflicts in CET 2. The same applies if two or more sources feed the same CITS.

Note: The conflict detection and resolution is not triggered by updates having occurred at the target, which is why this is not a master-master pattern. In this case, the trigger is that different updates occurred at two sources. However, the concepts described in *Master-Master Replication* still apply to solving this problem.

Resulting Context

This pattern inherits the benefits and liabilities from the *Data Replication* pattern and has the following additional benefits and liabilities:

Benefits

- **Source is freed from most of the replication load.** This is the most important benefit of a *Master-Slave Cascading Replication*. Only the first replication link adds load to the source. The remaining replication links do not burden the source. The CITS generally should not serve any applications so that conflicting operational demands between applications and replication services can be avoided.

- **CETs can be relatively autonomous.** Using a CET is a good way to provide data to other organizations because you can pass raw data on to the organizations and they can use the data however they want. Because you cannot force another organization to pull the data frequently, though, this could impact your source database system (for example, if the organization connected to your database directly). *Master-Slave Cascading Replication* liberates the source from this impact; a CITS is more appropriate to handle the impact because it does not serve any applications.

- **Adding more targets does not impact the source.** As your business requires more CETs you can add them without overburdening the source.

Liabilities

- **Increased latency.** Because the chains from the source to the targets are longer compared to direct replication, the delays in getting the replication set to the CETs can increase. Most implementations of this pattern use an immediate replication on the replication links to minimize this liability.

- **Potential for decreased availability.** The longer chains from the source to the targets have an impact on the overall availability as well. As the number of links in the chain increases, the opportunity for failures increases. You can address this liability by adding a second CITS and alternative chains in case of failures. A second CITS also offers the opportunity for load balancing by connecting half of the targets to each of the CITSs.

- **Additional administration and management.** *Master-Slave Cascading Replication* adds databases and replication links that must be administrated and managed. The whole replication environment should be controlled by management tools for an automatic surveillance of the ongoing operation.

- **Extra storage cost.** The CITS will add storage requirements to the overall environment.
- **Additional change management.** Structural changes to the source or the CETs require more attention because the CITS have to be adjusted appropriately. You should precisely plan and design the changes on all affected databases.

Operational Considerations

By applying *Master-Slave Cascading Replication,* most of the replication overhead is loaded on the CITS. Hence, it is common practice that the CITSs do not serve any applications. Instead, the applications are connected to the source and the targets only. All applications requiring write access of the database must be connected to the source.

Related Patterns

For more information, see the following related patterns:

Patterns That May Have Led You Here

- *Move Copy of Data.* This is the root pattern of this cluster. It presents the fundamental data movement building block that consists of source, data movement set, data movement link, and target. Transmissions in such a data movement building block are done asynchronously (or eventually) after the update of the source. Thus, the target applications must tolerate a certain amount of latency until changes are delivered.
- *Data Replication.* This pattern presents the architecture of a replication.
- *Master-Slave Replication.* This pattern presents the solution for a replication where the changes are replicated to the target without taking changes of the target into account. It will eventually overwrite any changes on the target.

Patterns That You Can Use Next

- *Implementing Master-Slave Transactional Incremental Replication Using SQL Server.*

Other Patterns of Interest

- *Master-Slave Snapshot Replication.* This pattern presents a solution that transmits the whole replication set from the source to the target on each transmission.
- *Master-Slave Transactional Incremental Replication.* This pattern presents a solution that transmits only the changes from the source to the target on a transaction-by-transaction basis.

Appendix

A

Patterns and Pattlets

Pattlets are actual patterns to which this guide refers, but does not discuss in detail. For more information about why pattlets are used, see Chapter 2, "Organizing Patterns." The following table lists each pattern and pattlet mentioned in this guide.

Table A.1: Patterns and Pattlets

Pattern or Pattlet Name	Problem Description	Solution Description
Maintain Data Copies (pattlet)	What proven architectural approach should you follow to maintain the content of data that exists in more than one place?	This root pattlet sets the context for the pattern cluster overall. The context is that you have, or are about to create, more than one copy of some data. The general solution is to either synchronously write to the copies from the originating application, or to synchronously post data to a local cache for later movement by an asynchronous service. The timeliness of that movement is given by the requirements of the applications.
Application-Managed Data Copies (pattlet)	What proven architectural approach should you follow to design synchronous data management services when you have data held in more than one data stores that are serving applications?	In this case, when a particular application makes a change to its copy of the data, it should then also make changes to the other copies. The application ensures that copies of the data and/or derived data are updated in the same transaction that changed the original data.

(continued)

Pattern or Pattlet Name	Problem Description	Solution Description
Move Copy of Data	What proven architectural approach should you follow to design data movement services when you have data held in data stores that are serving applications, and now you want other applications to use copies of that data?	This is the root pattern for any type of asynchronous writing of copies of data. The pattern presents the fundamental data movement building block, which consists of source, data movement set, data movement link, and target. Transmissions in such a data movement building block are done asynchronously (or eventually) after the update of the source. Thus, the target applications must tolerate certain latency until changes are delivered.
Data Replication	What proven architectural approach should you follow to create nearly-identical copies of the data, and possibly also allow the copies to be updated at either the source or target with changes being reflected in each other?	This pattern presents a special type of data movement (replication) with a simple acquisition and manipulation of the data, but possibly a complex write. The complexity of the write generally arises from the need to update both source and target and to eventually exchange the changes to the counterpart.
Extract-Transform-Load (ETL) (pattlet)	What proven architectural approach should you follow to create copies of the data when data flows one-way to the target, but getting the data is complex and it needs to be changed a lot before it can be written to the target?	ETL is a type of data movement with possibly a complex acquisition from heterogeneous sources, and/or a complex manipulation with aggregation and cleansing, but always a simple write by overwriting any changes on the target
Master-Master Replication	How do you design a replication where the replication set is updateable at either end, the changes need to be transmitted to the other party, and any conflicts need to be detected and resolved?	This is bidirectional data replication between source and target. This includes conflict detection and resolution in order to handle concurrent updates to different copies of the same data in the same transmission interval.

Pattern or Pattlet Name	Problem Description	Solution Description
Master-Slave Replication	How do you design replication when the copy is read-only, or it may be updated but changes to the copied data are not transmitted back, and they may overwritten on a later replication transmission?	This is unidirectional data replication from a source to a target, with overwrite of the target data by the transmission.
Master-Master Row-Level Synchronization	How do you design a replication to transmit data from the source to the target and vice versa, when the same replication set is updateable on both sides and you want to resolve conflicts at the row level?	A specific master-master replication where conflict detection and resolution are done at a row level.
Master-Slave Snapshot Replication	How do you design a master-slave replication to copy the entire replication set so that it is consistent at a given point in time?	A specific master-slave replication where the complete replication set is acquired from the source, possibly manipulated and written to the target. This design is also used for incremental replications and synchronizations to create the first copy of the data to be maintained.
Capture Transaction Details	How do you design a recording of transactional information for all changes to a data store so you can use these as a source for replication?	Design of recording transactional information by means of handcrafted artifacts to be used in an incremental replication using transactional changes. Required if there is no database management system (DBMS) transaction log or if the transaction log cannot be used for any reasons.
Master-Slave Transactional Incremental Replication	How do you design a replication link to support the transmission of changes using transactional details and replaying them on the target while meeting all integrity constraints?	A specific master-slave replication that transmits transactional information from the source and applies it to the target. This ensures that changed data is available to applications only after dependent operations of the same transaction have been replicated as well.

(continued)

Pattern or Pattlet Name	Problem Description	Solution Description
Implementing Master-Master Row-Level Synchronization Using SQL Server	How do you implement this design using Microsoft® SQL Server™?	Guidance to implement synchronization with row-level conflict detection and resolution by means provided with SQL Server merge replication.
Implementing Master-Slave Snapshot Replication Using SQL Server	How do you implement this design using SQL Server?	Guidance to implement snapshot replication by means provided with SQL Server snapshot replication.
Implementing Master-Slave Transactional Incremental Replication Using SQL Server	How do you implement this design using SQL Server?	Guidance to implement incremental replication using transactional information by means provided with SQL Server transactional replication.
Topologies for Data Copies (pattlet)	What are the proven architectural approaches for creating a topology of data copies for deployments?	The architectural approaches to deploying data copies on several platforms.
Master-Slave Cascading Replication	How can you optimize the replication of a set of targets in a master-slave environment, and minimize the impact on the source?	A deployment design for master-slave replications, where the replication from a single source to several targets uses a concatenation of replication links with intermediary databases serving both as target and source. The copies are all related by a need for data from the source replication set.

Glossary

The following table defines terms that are used throughout Data Patterns:

Table 1: Definitions for Data Patterns

Term	Definition
Access profile	A description of the characteristics of how application queries access the data store, such as search condition, size of the result set, frequency, and required response time.
Acquire	A service that gets a movement set from a data source. Acquisition may be a simple one-step process, or it may a multi-step process. The Acquire can enrich the data by adding details (such as time the data was acquired) to allow for management of the overall data integrity. It can acquire the movement set from the data structures directly, or it can acquire the set from other caches where only data changes are stored. Typically these caches are either database management system (DBMS) log record stores, message queuing system stores, or user-written databases. Acquire must either collect all changes, in which case the ordering of the changes is vital so that they are written correctly by the Write service; or it must collect the net change, which is the final result of all the changes that have occurred to the set since the last transmission.
Aggregation	Creation of a compound record or element from individual records or elements, where a *record* is a collection of data elements in the data store. In relational terms, a record is a row, and *elements* are columns.
Asynchronous	A style of processing where an application posts a request for an event to occur and then continues without waiting for the event. A separate service will recognize the request and take responsibility for ensuring that the event occurs.
Cascading replication	A hierarchical assembly of replication building blocks used for related replication transmissions. In this structure, the source(s) replicate to intermediary targets (of which there may be several layers). The intermediaries switch roles and become sources for the next replication link. This process continues until the replicated data reaches the end target. This configuration is used to reduce workload on the source when there are many end targets that all want the same replication set or a very similar replication set.

(continued)

Term	Definition
Composite movement set	A collection of one or more movement sets. Data in a composite movement set can come from one or more data stores. In a data store, the subset that is to be be moved is a movement set. The sum of these movement sets is called a composite movement set and comprises all the data you want to move to the application. Composite movement sets are usually relevant to *Extract-Transform-Load* (*ETL*). **Source 1** Mvmt. Set **Composite Movement Set** Mvmt. Set **Source 2**
Conflict	A conflict arises whenever two or more copies of the same data are independently updated in a time interval. Conflicts are detected only when one of the copies replicates its data to the other copy and the Write service discovers that the other copy of the data has been changed since the last replication. The conflict must be resolved by the Write service.
Conflict detection	The process of detecting conflicting change transactions on the common data in a source and target during a transmission.
Conflict resolution	The process of resolving conflicting change transactions on the common data in a source and target during a transmission. The resolution method specifies whether the source or the target change should overrule the other; or it may return data as an aggregated result of the conflicting transactions; or it may require manual intervention to resolve some conflicts, for example, those where complex business rules need to be invoked.
Data movement	The act of reliably and repeatedly moving a copy of data from its current physical location(s) to different location(s) and possibly transforming its contents. This action requires several architectural components that are described in the patterns, and a process that is outside the scope of these patterns.

Term	Definition
Data movement building block	The fundamental architectural building block for data movement. This block is used to assemble all solutions that move data copies to the applications that need them. It consists of a source, a movement set, a data movement link, and a target data store.
Data movement link	A connection between the source and target along which the relevant source movement set moves from one data store to another with appropriate security. This link includes the method of transmission of data at each step that moves the data (which includes any needed intermediary transient data stores). The data movement link also includes the Acquire, Manipulate, and Write replication services.
Database	A collection of data managed by a DBMS. The scope of the term *database* can vary depending on the DBMS product used. For clarity, these patterns use the term as defined by Microsoft® SQL Server™.
Full replication	A replication in which a whole replication set of complete rows is moved from the source to the target on every transmission through a replication link. (A full replication is also called a *snapshot replication*.)
Immediate replication	A replication in which every change to the source triggers a replication transmission to the target. When using a database, the changes will be transmitted immediately after the changing transaction commits its changes to the DBMS.
Incremental replication	A replication in which the replication set consists of only the changes that have been made to rows since the last transmission are sent (as opposed to the complete replication set). When designing an incremental replication, you need to decide whether to send all changes that have occurred to any particular record during the replication interval, or whether to send only the net effect of those changes.
Key updates	Changes to the primary key of a database record, such as SQL updates to the columns of the table key within a replication set. The replication must handle such key updates with special care.
Manipulate	A service that changes the content or form of the movement set in some way and passes it on in a format that can easily be written to the target. Manipulations can vary in complexity from a null event (where Manipulate does not change the data) to very radical data alternations.

(continued)

Term	Definition
Master-master	A source-target relationship in which the replication set can be changed at either the source or the target within a replication interval, and these changes are to be posted back to the other party on the next transmission in its direction. Thus the source and target are equals with respect to rights to make changes to the replication set. (Master-master replication is also known as *peer-to-peer* replication.) The write logic of a replication link must include logic for resolving multiple-updater conflicts, and two replication links must exist between the peers since they will swap source and target roles when exchanging data (see following figure).

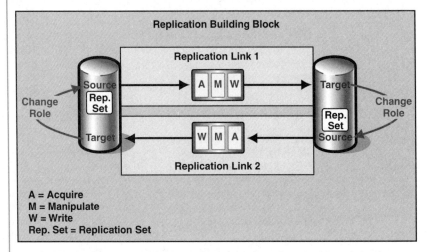

Replication Building Block

Replication Link 1

Replication Link 2

A = Acquire
M = Manipulate
W = Write
Rep. Set = Replication Set

The Master-master relationship should not be confused with a pair of master-slave relationships between source and target. Although the configurations look similar, the pair of master-slave relationships does not provide the capability to update a common set of data at either end (see following figure).

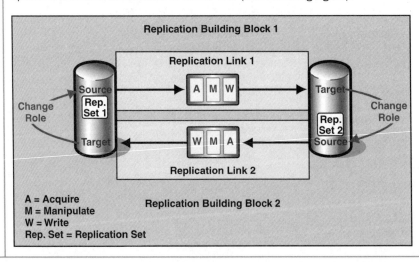

Replication Building Block 1

Replication Link 1

Replication Link 2

A = Acquire
M = Manipulate
W = Write
Rep. Set = Replication Set

Replication Building Block 2

Term	Definition
Master-slave	A source-target relationship in which the source replication set is written to the target without checking for conflicts. Either the replication data at the target data store is read-only; or any updates to the replication data from the source are not to be copied back to the source database and the changes can be overwritten by a later replication transmission. **Replication Building Block** Rep. Set — Source — Replication Link — A M W — Target **A = Acquire** **M = Manipulate** **W = Write** **Rep. Set = Replication Set**
Movement set	An identified subset of data that exists within a single source. A movement set is copied from that source and is sent across a data movement link to one or more targets. During the copy operation, the content and form of the movement set may change as it is acquired, manipulated, and written.
On-demand replication	A replication in which transmissions are started by explicit operator request, as opposed to being triggered or scheduled by an automated process.
Operation	An action performed on a row of data, such as an INSERT, UPDATE, or DELETE operation.
Optimistic concurrency control	A data integrity technique that allows multiple parties to update different copies of the same set of data. When the changes are merged, a check is done to see if the changes affected the same data within the data store. If such a conflict is detected, it must be resolved by a defined method; for example, the more recent change overrules any older changes.
Pattern	A three-part relationship between a general problem, its context, and its solution, which is based on real-world experience and is documented in a consistent, formal structure. A pattern encapsulates experienced practitioner knowledge and can be used as a starting place for creating solutions to specific situational problems.
Pattlet	A placeholder for a pattern where there is good cause to believe that a pattern exists that has not yet been written. Usually expressed as a name, and a problem or solution statement, or both.
Periodical replication	A replication in which transmissions are scheduled to be run at a fixed time or after a fixed interval.

(continued)

Term	Definition
Pessimistic concurrency control	A data integrity technique that requires an application to acquire a data lock before it can change data. This means that only a single party can change the data at any point in time.
Projection	A selected subset of columns from tables. If the replication set is not a full replication, then it is a projection.
Publication	The Microsoft SQL Server term for a set of data made available for replication by a publisher.
Publisher	In Microsoft SQL Server, the role of a platform that provides the source for a replication link.
Push replication	Replication that is invoked at the source.
Pull replication	Replication that is invoked at the target.
Redundant data	Any data that does not provide new information but already exists elsewhere in the environment as an exact copy or is derived by more complex manipulations, such as aggregations.
Related replication links	Replication links that require information about one another's actions because of the relationship they support between the source and target. Master-master replication uses two related replication links between source and target in opposite directions to allow changes to the replicated data at either end, and to transmit the changes to the counterpart.
Replication	The act of reliably and repeatedly moving a copy of a set of data from its current physical location(s) to different location(s). If both source and target have updated the replicated data since the last replication transmission, the process of writing the data to the target may be complex. Otherwise, the process of moving the data is very simple.
Replication building block	The fundamental architectural building block for replication. This block serves as the basis for all replication solutions. It consists of a source replication set to be replicated, a replication link, and a target database.
Replication interval	The period of time between replication transmissions.
Replication link	A connection between the source and target along which the relevant source replication set can be moved from one database to another with appropriate security. This link includes the method of transmission of data at each step that moves the data (which includes any needed intermediary, transient data stores). The replication link also includes the Acquire, Manipulate, and Write replication services.
Replication set	A movement set that is used for data replication. A replication set consists of one or more replication units.
Replication transmission	The act of moving a replication set from source to target.

Term	Definition
Replication unit	The smallest amount of data that can be discretely recognized in a transmission. The replication unit can be one of the following: • The complete replication set • A table in the replication set • A transaction • A row (of a table in the replication set) • A column (of a row in a table in the replication set)
Snapshot replication	A replication in which a whole replication set is moved from the source to the target on every transmission through a replication link. (A snapshot replication is also called a *full replication*.)
Source	The data store that contains a movement set to be replicated.
Subscriber	In Microsoft SQL Server, the role of a platform that acts as the target for a replication link.
Subscription	In Microsoft SQL Server, the metadata that defines a replication set.
Synchronization	The process of replicating and applying changes from a source to a target when data from the replication set may potentially have been updated at both ends, and these conflicts need to be detected and resolved.
Synchronization building block	A refinement of the replication building block consisting of two replication links and a synchronization controller. The controller manages the synchronization and relates the replication link pair.
Synchronous	A style of processing where an application requests that an event occurs and waits for the event to complete, so that the application is certain of the result of its request before it proceeds. In the case of data operations, it means performing a set of data operations within a common unit of work as defined by DBMS commit services so that the state of the set of data is certain.
Target	The data store in a data movement building block where the copy data is written.
Topology	A layout of related data movement building blocks that provides a map of the source and target data stores and the links between them. By describing the relationships between these elements, a topology helps you to determine the provenance of the movement set and assess the impact of changes to the data movement set or to the configuration of the movement building blocks.
Transaction	A collection of one or more manipulations of a database. A transaction should adhere to the ACID principles: Atomicity, Consistency, Isolation, and Durability.
Transaction log	A special data store provided by a DBMS that allows copies of transactional database changes to be persisted to a location other than the data store itself. A transaction log's primary purpose is to allow a DBMS to recover from failures.
Transactional Replication	A type of incremental replication in which the replication unit is a transaction.

(continued)

Term	Definition
Transform	Transform is a service of the complex data movement process commonly known as ETL (Extract-Transform-Load).
Transmission	The process of moving of the movement set from source to target according to defined functional and operational requirements.
Trigger	A database object attached to a table that invokes additional actions on behalf of an initiating operation. The common usage of a trigger is to perform additional actions on certain kinds of manipulations and to free the application from the implementation of these actions.
Write	A service that writes a movement set to the target data store(s). Write deals with any errors returned from the attempted write, which may be simple (such as database error codes) or more complex (such as multiple-updater conflicts).

patterns & practices

About Microsoft *patterns & practices*

Microsoft *patterns & practices* guides contain specific recommendations illustrating how to design, build, deploy, and operate architecturally sound solutions to challenging business and technical scenarios. They offer deep technical guidance based on real-world experience that goes far beyond white papers to help enterprise IT professionals, information workers, and developers quickly deliver sound solutions.

IT Professionals, information workers, and developers can choose from four types of *patterns & practices*:

- **Patterns**—Patterns are a consistent way of documenting solutions to commonly occurring problems. Patterns are available that address specific architecture, design, and implementation problems. Each pattern also has an associated GotDotNet Community.

- **Reference Architectures**—Reference Architectures are IT system-level architectures that address the business requirements, LifeCycle requirements, and technical constraints for commonly occurring scenarios. Reference Architectures focus on planning the architecture of IT systems.

- **Reference Building Blocks and IT Services**—References Building Blocks and IT Services are re-usable sub-system designs that address common technical challenges across a wide range of scenarios. Many include tested reference implementations to accelerate development. Reference Building Blocks and IT Services focus on the design and implementation of sub-systems.

- **Lifecycle Practices**—Lifecycle Practices provide guidance for tasks outside the scope of architecture and design such as deployment and operations in a production environment.

Patterns & practices guides are reviewed and approved by Microsoft engineering teams, consultants, Product Support Services, and by partners and customers. *Patterns & practices* guides are:

- **Proven**—They are based on field experience.
- **Authoritative**—They offer the best advice available.
- **Accurate**—They are technically validated and tested.
- **Actionable**—They provide the steps to success.
- **Relevant**—They address real-world problems based on customer scenarios.

Patterns & practices guides are designed to help IT professionals, information workers, and developers:

Reduce project cost

- Exploit the Microsoft engineering efforts to save time and money on your projects.
- Follow the Microsoft recommendations to lower your project risk and achieve predictable outcomes.

Increase confidence in solutions

- Build your solutions on proven Microsoft recommendations so you can have total confidence in your results.
- Rely on thoroughly tested and supported guidance, but production quality recommendations and code, not just samples.

Deliver strategic IT advantage

- Solve your problems today and take advantage of future Microsoft technologies with practical advice.

patterns & practices: Current Titles

October 2003

Title	Link to Online Version	Book
Patterns		
Enterprise Solution Patterns using Microsoft .NET	http://msdn.microsoft.com/practices/type/Patterns /Enterprise/default.asp	
Microsoft Data Patterns	http://msdn.microsoft.com/practices/type/Patterns /Data/default.asp	
Reference Architectures		
Application Architecture for .NET: Designing Applications and Services	http://msdn.microsoft.com/library/default.asp?url= /library/en-us/dnbda/html/distapp.asp	
Enterprise Notification Reference Architecture for Exchange 2000 Server	http://msdn.microsoft.com/library/default.asp?url= /library/en-us/dnentdevgen/html/enraelp.asp	
Improving Web Application Security: Threats and Countermeasures	http://msdn.microsoft.com/library/default.asp?url= /library/en-us/dnnetsec/html/ThreatCounter.asp	
Microsoft Accelerator for Six Sigma	http://www.microsoft.com/technet/treeview /default.asp?url=/technet/itsolutions/mso/sixsigma /default.asp	
Microsoft Active Directory Branch Office Guide: Volume 1: Planning	http://www.microsoft.com/technet/treeview /default.asp?url=/technet/prodtechnol/ad /windows2000/deploy/adguide/default.asp	
Microsoft Active Directory Branch Office Series Volume 2: Deployment and Operations	http://www.microsoft.com/technet/treeview /default.asp?url=/technet/prodtechnol/ad /windows2000/deploy/adguide/default.asp	
Microsoft Content Integration Pack for Content Management Server 2001 and SharePoint Portal Server 2001	http://msdn.microsoft.com/library/default.asp?url= /library/en-us/dncip/html/cip.asp	
Microsoft Exchange 2000 Server Hosting Series Volume 1: Planning	Online Version not available	
Microsoft Exchange 2000 Server Hosting Series Volume 2: Deployment	Online Version not available	

Title	Link to Online Version	Book
Microsoft Exchange 2000 Server Upgrade Series Volume 1: Planning	*http://www.microsoft.com/technet/treeview /default.asp?url=/technet/itsolutions/guide /default.asp*	
Microsoft Exchange 2000 Server Upgrade Series Volume 2: Deployment	http://www.microsoft.com/technet/treeview /default.asp?url=/technet/itsolutions/guide /default.asp	
Microsoft Solution for Intranets	*http://www.microsoft.com/technet/treeview /default.asp?url=/technet/itsolutions/mso /msi/Default.asp*	
Microsoft Solution for Securing Wireless LANs	*http://www.microsoft.com/downloads /details.aspx?FamilyId=CDB639B3-010B-47E7-B23 4-A27CDA291DAD&displaylang=en*	
Microsoft Systems Architecture— Enterprise Data Center	*http://www.microsoft.com/technet/treeview /default.asp?url=/technet/itsolutions/edc /Default.asp*	
Microsoft Systems Architecture— Internet Data Center	*http://www.microsoft.com/technet/treeview/ default.asp?url=/technet/itsolutions/idc/default.asp*	
The Enterprise Project Management Solution	*http://www.microsoft.com/technet/treeview /default.asp?url=/technet/itsolutions/mso/epm /default.asp*	
UNIX Application Migration Guide	*http://msdn.microsoft.com/library/default.asp?url= /library/en-us/dnucmg/html/ucmglp.asp*	
Reference Building Blocks and IT Services		
.NET Data Access Architecture Guide	*http://msdn.microsoft.com/library/default.asp?url= /library/en-us/dnbda/html/daag.asp*	
Application Updater Application Block	*http://msdn.microsoft.com/library/default.asp?url= /library/en-us/dnbda/html/updater.asp*	
Asynchronous Invocation Application Block	*http://msdn.microsoft.com/library/default.asp?url= /library/en-us/dnpag/html/paiblock.asp*	
Authentication in ASP.NET: .NET Security Guidance	*http://msdn.microsoft.com/library/default.asp?url= /library/en-us/dnbda/html/authaspdotnet.asp*	
Building Interoperable Web Services: WS-I Basic Profile 1.0	*http://msdn.microsoft.com/library/default.asp?url= /library/en-us/dnsvcinter/html/wsi-bp_msdn_ landingpage.asp*	
Building Secure ASP.NET Applications: Authentication, Authorization, and Secure Communication	*http://msdn.microsoft.com/library/default.asp?url= /library/en-us/dnnetsec/html/secnetlpMSDN.asp*	

Title	Link to Online Version	Book
Caching Application Block	*http://msdn.microsoft.com/library/default.asp?url= /library/en-us/dnpag/html/Cachingblock.asp*	
Caching Architecture Guide for .Net Framework Applications	*http://msdn.microsoft.com/library/default.asp?url= /library/en-us/dnbda/html/CachingArch.asp?frame= true*	
Configuration Management Application Block	*http://msdn.microsoft.com/library/default.asp?url= /library/en-us/dnbda/html/cmab.asp*	
Data Access Application Block for .NET	*http://msdn.microsoft.com/library/default.asp?url= /library/en-us/dnbda/html/daab-rm.asp*	
Designing Application-Managed Authorization	*http://msdn.microsoft.com/library/?url=/library /en-us/dnbda/html/damaz.asp*	
Designing Data Tier Components and Passing Data Through Tiers	*http://msdn.microsoft.com/library/default.asp?url= /library/en-us/dnbda/html/BOAGag.asp*	
Exception Management Application Block for .NET	*http://msdn.microsoft.com/library/default.asp?url= /library/en-us/dnbda/html/emab-rm.asp*	
Exception Management Architecture Guide	*http://msdn.microsoft.com/library/default.asp?url= /library/en-us/dnbda/html/exceptdotnet.asp*	
Microsoft .NET/COM Migration and Interoperability	*http://msdn.microsoft.com/library/default.asp?url= /library/en-us/dnbda/html/cominterop.asp*	
Microsoft Windows Server 2003 Security Guide	*http://www.microsoft.com/downloads/ details.aspx?FamilyId=8A2643C1-0685-4D89-B655- 521EA6C7B4DB&displaylang=en*	
Monitoring in .NET Distributed Application Design	*http://msdn.microsoft.com/library/default.asp?url= /library/en-us/dnbda/html/monitordotnet.asp*	
New Application Installation using Systems Management Server	*http://www.microsoft.com/business/reducecosts /efficiency/manageability/application.mspx*	
Patch Management using Microsoft Systems Management Server - Operations Guide	*http://www.microsoft.com/technet/treeview/ default.asp?url=/technet/itsolutions/msm/swdist/ pmsms/pmsmsog.asp*	
Patch Management Using Microsoft Software Update Services - Operations Guide	*http://www.microsoft.com/technet/treeview/ default.asp?url=/technet/itsolutions/msm/swdist/ pmsus/pmsusog.asp*	
Service Aggregation Application Block	*http://msdn.microsoft.com/library/default.asp?url= /library/en-us/dnpag/html/serviceagg.asp*	
Service Monitoring and Control using Microsoft Operations Manager	*http://www.microsoft.com/business/reducecosts /efficiency/manageability/monitoring.mspx*	

Title	Link to Online Version	Book
User Interface Process Application Block	http://msdn.microsoft.com/library/default.asp?url= /library/en-us/dnbda/html/uip.asp	
Web Service Façade for Legacy Applications	http://msdn.microsoft.com/library/default.asp?url= /library/en-us/dnpag/html/wsfacadelegacyapp.asp	
Lifecycle Practices		
Backup and Restore for Internet Data Center	http://www.microsoft.com/technet/treeview/default.asp ?url=/technet/ittasks/maintain/backuprest/Default.asp	
Deploying .NET Applications: Lifecycle Guide	http://msdn.microsoft.com/library/default.asp?url= /library/en-us/dnbda/html/DALGRoadmap.asp	
Microsoft Exchange 2000 Server Operations Guide	http://www.microsoft.com/technet/treeview/default. asp?url=/technet/prodtechnol/exchange/exchange 2000/maintain/operate/opsguide/default.asp	
Microsoft SQL Server 2000 High Availability Series: Volume 1: Planning	http://www.microsoft.com/technet/treeview /default.asp?url=/technet/prodtechnol/sql/deploy /confeat/sqlha/SQLHALP.asp	
Microsoft SQL Server 2000 High Availability Series: Volume 2: Deployment	http://www.microsoft.com/technet/treeview /default.asp?url=/technet/prodtechnol/sql/deploy /confeat/sqlha/SQLHALP.asp	
Microsoft SQL Server 2000 Operations Guide	http://www.microsoft.com/technet/treeview /default.asp?url=/technet/prodtechnol/sql/maintain /operate/opsguide/default.asp	
Operating .NET-Based Applications	http://www.microsoft.com/technet/treeview /default.asp?url=/technet/itsolutions/nct/maintain /opnetapp/default.asp	
Production Debugging for .NET-Connected Applications	http://msdn.microsoft.com/library/default.asp?url= /library/en-us/dnbda/html/DBGrm.asp	
Security Operations for Microsoft Windows 2000 Server	http://www.microsoft.com/technet/treeview /default.asp?url=/technet/security/prodtech /win2000/secwin2k/default.asp	
Security Operations Guide for Exchange 2000 Server	http://www.microsoft.com/technet/treeview /default.asp?url=/technet/security/prodtech /mailexch/opsguide/default.asp	
Team Development with Visual Studio .NET and Visual SourceSafe	http://msdn.microsoft.com/library/default.asp?url= /library/en-us/dnbda/html/tdlg_rm.asp	

 This title is available as a Book